W9-CND-486

The Aesthetic Movement

The Aesthetic Movement

ELIZABETH ASLIN

Prelude to Art Nouveau

EXCALIBUR BOOKS
NEW YORK

Copyright © 1969 by Elizabeth Aslin

First published in USA 1981
by Excalibur Books
Excalibur is a trademark of Simon & Schuster
Distributed by Bookthrift
New York, New York

ALL RIGHTS RESERVED

ISBN 0-89673-097-2

Printed in Hong Kong by South China Printing Co.

Contents

List of plates

List of figures in the text

Chapter 1

INTRODUCTION

In recent years, despite the popularity of certain aspects of Victorian art, the belief has grown that the Victorian period as a whole was a Philistine age in which the low standards in all the visual arts was relieved only by the work of William Morris and that *fin de siècle* Art Nouveau, with its own brand of poetic gloom, heralded the dawn of the enlightenment of the twentieth century. Admittedly a high proportion of what was produced in England during the nineteenth century in the fields of the decorative arts and of architecture was unattractive, but this oversimplification is open to question on at least two grounds. It presupposes that the work of the twentieth century is of necessity superior to that of our immediate forebears and it completely ignores the genuine modern style of the Victorians, the Art or Aesthetic Movement of the eighteen-seventies and 'eighties when it could be said that 'there has assuredly never been since the world began an age in which people thought, talked, wrote and spent such inordinate sums of money and hours of time in cultivating and indulging their tastes'.[1]

The movement, beginning with the work of a few architects and designers in the 'sixties, gathered force until, in the 'eighties, it embraced every art form from the greetings card to domestic architecture. It introduced Japanese art to children's story books and red brick Queen Anne architecture to the streets of London; it led to changes in fashionable dress, to the first garden suburb and to the vogue for painted dark green or Venetian red front doors and railings which lasted for half a century in England. People described themselves as 'going in' for 'High Art', for Art Decoration, Art Embroidery or Art Furniture, this last expression becoming so general that by the mid 'seventies the *London Trades Directory* lists 'Art Furniture Manufacturers' quite separately from ordinary cabinet-makers and furnishers. The tone of the whole movement is recorded in a conversation which William Morris had with a lady who said, 'You know I wouldn't mind a lad being a cabinet-maker if he only made Art Furniture'.[2]

In terms of architecture and the applied arts the movement was confined to the English-speaking countries, that is to the British Isles and the United States, though it would seem that the fashion for aesthetic clothing spread briefly to France, in the early eighteen-eighties. By this time 'aesthetic', a word virtually unknown in the early part of the century, had become the adjective for almost anything that was currently fashionable.

The term was invented or adapted from the Greek by the German philosopher Baumgarten whose work *Aesthetica* was published in 1750. The word, defined as meaning the science of the beautiful or the philosophy of taste, was brought to England at the beginning of the nineteenth century together with its opposite, 'philistine', which in this context meant one deficient in liberal culture whose interests were bounded by material and commonplace things as opposed to the high-minded spiritual and artistic values of the aesthetes. By the middle of the century the two terms were in general if somewhat ill-defined use. The naturalist, Charles Darwin, for instance, described birds as aesthetic, meaning that in his view their taste for beauty was similar to that of man, while another writer thought that the term aesthetic covered 'the adoption of a sentimental archaism as the ideal of beauty'. By 1880, however, the Aesthetic Movement in the arts was a well-established fact and the name itself part of everyday speech.

One of the origins of the movement, and that to which its name can be attributed, was to be found in a long-standing literary and philosophical dispute as to whether an object was actually beautiful in itself or whether it merely appeared so to those whose sensibilities and training enabled them to appreciate it. Assuming the latter to be the case it was obviously necessary to establish principles or standards by which the beauty of any work of art or domestic utensil could be assessed and 'hence', wrote a contemporary author, 'the essence of the movement is the union of persons of cultivated tastes to define and decide upon what is to be admired'.[3] This meant that in the centre of the movement there was a closely-knit group of self-appointed *cognoscenti* with carefully cultivated sensibilities and that some sort of publicity was needed by them to pass on to their followers the standards to which they should aspire. Aesthetes laid down standards of colour, of ornament and of form for all aspects of art and domestic decoration which, reduced to the basic essentials, were simple, sensible and a considerable improvement on the elaborations of the design of the High Victorian period. The public, however, naturally tended to associate aesthetic ideas with the more extreme elements in the movement and this led to a great deal of simple fun and even ridicule in the press which obscured the overall serious and significant effects which influenced many aspects of everyday life. These benefits were explained in an article in the short-lived periodical *The Burlington*, sub-titled 'A High Class Monthly Periodical', which was the mouthpiece of the movement in 1881 and 1882. Having dealt with the recent improvements in the costume of an imaginary Mrs Jones, the author proceeds to Mr Philistine Jones who

'dubs all aesthetes idiots, while he also adopts their ideas. A dozen years ago his dazzling carpets and wallpapers were enough to give a templar a fit of delirium tremens – his furniture was a roughly hewn mass of ponderous mahogany, his walls were hung with abominations encircled in tawdry gilt frames – which he called pictures, he delighted in waxen fruit under glass covers; his crockery, his glass, in fine everything he possessed and especially admired, was a violation of good taste. But some-how he has changed all this – the human eye may now repose upon the neutral tints of his carpets and walls. He has a dado, and blue and white china may be espied in nooks and corners – he has eschewed gilt – he has ceased to care for stucco – he lives in a Queen Anne house and actually has begun to think about the shape of his jugs.

'This improvement is rapidly spreading through all classes of society – good taste is no longer an expensive luxury to indulge in – the commonest articles of domestic use are now fashioned in accordance with its laws and the poorest may have in their homes at the cost of a few pence cups and saucers and jugs and teapots, more artistic in form and design than were to be found twenty years ago in any homes but those of the cultured rich.

'And to whom are we indebted for these advantages? Why, to the Aesthetes, the fools and idiots of Philistine phraseology.'

Even allowing for the exaggerations of an enthusiast such sweeping changes, which were also recorded by other writers, must obviously have been based on something more than the fancies of a few artistic cranks and exhibitionists whose languid manner, based on the drooping figures of Burne-Jones, disguised a sincere attempt to bring some beauty into an increasingly ugly world. Despite the reforming spirit which inspired both designers and writers on the decorative arts, this beauty took diverse forms and the unifying element of the movement was one of mood and atmosphere rather than any immediately obvious common visual quality. Each designer strove for a practical interpretation of the new ideas which at the same time was personally satisfying.

The actual artistic origins of the movement were far more complex than something compounded of these abstract theories and a feeling for Burne-Jones, and they date back to the beginning of Queen Victoria's reign, if not even earlier. In the eighteen-thirties and 'forties it was fairly generally agreed by thinking men that English design in all branches of the industrial arts was at a very low ebb. Ornament was lavish and overwrought and the exciting possibilities of new materials, new industrial processes, new dye-stuffs for fabric printing and, above all, an expanding market merely led manufacturers to the indiscriminate production of ever increasing quantities of singularly ill-designed and elaborate objects. Design motifs were picked at random from the many published 'cribs' the most distinguished of which, Owen Jones' *Grammar of Ornament*, contained examples of every known historical style. Eclecticism was rampant and the simple elegances of the eighteenth century were scorned. It was not only those professionally involved, such as artists and designers, but other public-spirited men who became alarmed at design standards and addressed themselves to matters of taste and in particular to the form and type of decoration and ornament. In early Victorian terms this problem was one of how to apply 'art' to industrial products.

Henry Cole (1808–82) was an early and influential reformer who later became the moving influence behind the Great Exhibition of 1851 and the first head of the South Kensington Museum. Cole's remedy was the employment of painters and sculptors to design objects of everyday use. He also recommended the use of naturalistic 'appropriate' ornament. This meant that instead of the indiscriminate use of design motifs culled from a variety of historical sources, designers were to confine themselves to renderings of natural forms which symbolized the use of the object in question. Thus ears of corn were suitable for bread boards, bunches of grapes for wine jugs and hops for beer tankards, irrespective of the material used. Appropriate ornament became a popular form of early-Victorian decoration but obviously it had little effect on the basic shape of the objects, as opposed to the ornament applied to them.

The average manufacturer's panacea for these design ills was to make strenuous efforts to emulate the French both in design and quality of manufacture. This was not a piece of disinterested idealism but a practical attempt to increase exports and reduce imports; as French goods were popular so it seemed sensible to imitate them. It was no doubt with this aim in mind that the first exhibits purchased for what is now the Victoria and Albert Museum were objects selected from the Paris Exhibition of French Industrial Arts held in 1844. These included examples of Sèvres porcelain, as well as elaborate pieces of metalwork, and they were intended as models for British manufacturers and artisans; they seem to have achieved the required effect all too thoroughly. Reporting to the Select Committee on the School of Design in 1849, Henry Cole said that 'the best of our metal ornamental designs are plagiarisms from the French; as respects the Potteries, the best of the pottery are imitations of old Dresden and Sèvres designs' and the list continues through all the other categories of industrial design. Another witness on the same occasion stated that all the English wallpapers were direct copies from the French production. Fresh impetus was given to this trend by an influx of foreign artisans and tradesmen around 1848, particularly into the cabinet-making trade, and by 1851 almost all the English exhibits in the industrial design sections of the famous Great Exhibition of that year were based on French models, both in form and colour. Furniture was carved and gilt, metal mounts abounded, and rich, strident colours were used for carpets, textiles and wallpapers.

This imitation of French design continued through the 'fifties although efforts were made through various Select Committees, Government Reports and, above all, Exhibitions held up and down the country to improve public taste and native design standards. A small victory was won for England by a very large exhibit at the Paris International Exhibition of 1855. On this occasion, despite the reported 'incontestable pre-eminence of France in many sections'[4] an English cabinet-making firm won an award for a giant buffet or sideboard. Even this was in the style of Louis XVI and designed by a Frenchman though made by English craftsmen, no less than forty of whom laboured to produce this small English triumph. The real turning point came with the International Exhibition held in London in 1862. Less well-known than the earlier Great Exhibition, it was of infinitely greater significance in the development of nineteenth-century taste and design. In all the contemporary writing on that exhibition there was a remarkable self-congratulatory tone admitting by implication the previously unsatisfactory state of affairs. 'It is a pleasure to report a most unmistakable advance in almost every direction since the exhibition of

1 Corner cupboard; ebonized wood with incised decoration designed by Alfred Waterhouse and painted in colours on a gilt ground by Mrs Alfred Waterhouse, 1878. *London, Victoria and Albert Museum.*

2   Buffet in ebonized wood with silver-plated fittings and inset panels of embossed Japanese leather paper, designed by E. W. Godwin, 1867. *London, Victoria and Albert Museum.*

3   Sideboard in various woods with metal mounts designed by Alfred Waterhouse, about 1872. *The Rt Hon. the Earl of Selborne.*

4   Chair, with turned and ebonized decoration, designed by Alfred Waterhouse, 1872. *The Rt Hon. the Earl of Selborne.*

5   Armchair in ebonized wood with rush seat combining Japanese and English traditional design, about 1870. *The Rev. Michael McLean.*

6   Side chair in golden oak, 'Eastlake' style, about 1880. *Ne York ; Courtesy of the Brooklyn Museum ; Gift of Mrs Otto Gretze*

2

3

4

6

7 Buffet of ebony, with marquetry of various woods and carved boxwood panels, designed by B. J. Talbert and made by Gillow's, 1873. *Vienna, Österreichisches Museum für Angewandte Kunst.*

8 Detail of plate 7 above.

9 Original design for 'Sunflower' wallpaper by B. J. Talbert. The wallpaper was made by Jeffrey & Co., 1878. *London, Victoria and Albert Museum.*

10 'Apple Blossom', hand-printed wallpaper designed by Lewis F. Day, 1878, and made by Jeffrey & Co., for W. B. Simpson & Sons. *London, Victoria and Albert Museum.*

11 'Trellis dado', hand-printed wallpaper designed by Lewis F. Day for W. B. Simpson & Sons, about 1877. *London, Victoria and Albert Museum.*

7

8

14

15

On previous page

12 Wallpaper designed by B. J. Talbert and exhibited by Jeffrey & Co., Paris 1878. *London, Victoria and Albert Museum.*

13 Wallpaper, frieze, filling and dado designed by B. J. Talbert and made by Jeffrey & Co., 1877. *London, Victoria and Albert Museum.*

14 'The Sleeping Beauty', machine-printed nursery wallpaper designed by Walter Crane and made by Jeffrey & Co., 1875. *London, Victoria and Albert Museum.*

15 Original design for part of 'Swan, Rush and Iris' dado, by Walter Crane. The paper was printed by Jeffrey & Co., 1877. *London, Victoria and Albert Museum.*

16

16 Original design for a wallpaper
by E. W. Godwin. The paper
was printed by Jeffrey & Co., 1872.
London, Victoria and Albert Museum.

17 Decorative panel in carved
boxwood from a piano designed by
H. W. Batley and made by James
Shoolbred & Co., 1878. *London,
Victoria and Albert Museum.*

17

18

18   Chair in ebonized wood with split-cane back and seat designed by E. W. Godwin and made by William Watt about 1877. *In the author's possession.*

19   'Jacobean' armchair made by Collier and Plucknett, Warwick, from a design by E. W. Godwin of about 1877. *London, Victoria and Albert Museum.*

20   Sussex chair of ebonized beech with a rush seat made by Morris & Co., from about 1865. *London, Victoria and Albert Museum.*   20

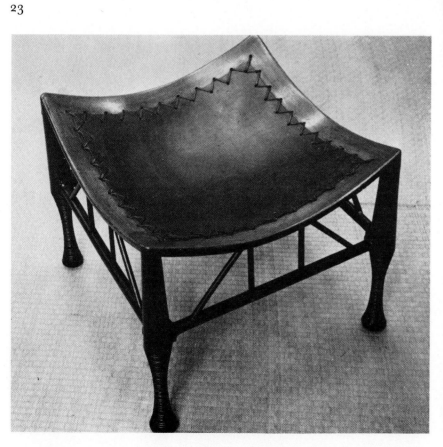

21

23

22

21 Table in ebonized oak, designed by E. W. Godwin and made by William Watt, 1876. This table was originally owned by Ellen Terry. *Bristol, City Art Gallery.*

22 Chair probably designed and made for Liberty & Co., 1884. *Walthamstow, William Morris Gallery.*

23 'The Thebes stool', in mahogany with a leather seat designed and made for Liberty & Co., 1884. *London, Victoria and Albert Museum.*

24   25

24   Chair and coffee table
designed by E. W. Godwin, 1875
and 1867 and made by William
Watt. *London, Victoria and Albert
Museum.*

25   Chairs with ebonized frames
and mahogany panels inlaid with
light wood. Part of a set of bedroom
furniture made by Herter Brothers
for William T. Carter of
Philadelphia, 1876. *Philadelphia,
Museum of Art.*

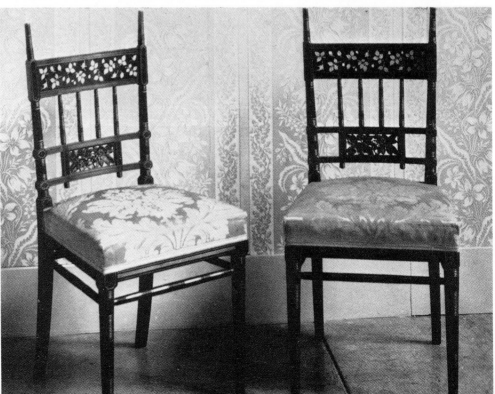

1851'[5] wrote one commentator, and others spoke of the disappearance of meaningless ornament and the development of a new lightness and grace in English work. In both learned professional journals and the popular press all were agreed that English designers and artisans had at last established themselves as the equals of their foreign rival in almost all trades.

In addition to this newly acquired self-confidence in English design and manufacture in the industrial arts, there appeared in the 1862 Exhibition other new elements which were to have a profound influence on later nineteenth-century taste. The first was that William Morris (1834–96) and the colleagues with whom he was associated in the newly-formed firm of Morris, Marshall, Faulkner and Company, exhibited publicly for the first time. Their painted furniture and rich embroideries had previously only been seen by close friends in the privacy of their homes. Now they were available to a wider audience and as Morris's associates included such men as Burne-Jones, Rossetti and Ford Madox Brown who painted on furniture at this date, Pre-Raphaelite painting reached a wider, new public. The second new influence was that of Japanese art which was to have a widespread effect on the domestic arts in the latter part of the Victorian period and was one of the most important contributory factors in the Aesthetic Movement. It was the first time that the Japanese had shown at one of the great European exhibitions and, although their display appears to have been quite small and rather cluttered by modern standards, the simplicity of the individual exhibits had a profound and inspiring effect on a small group of architects and painters whose own work eventually led to a mania for almost anything Japanese.

Thus the foundations on which the new 'Art' movement was built were first, a certain national self-confidence in design which made it unnecessary to play safe and emulate the French; secondly, there was the Pre-Raphaelite revolution against the false in painting accompanied by a similar revolt in the decorative arts against the false in decoration, a reformation which stressed the novel idea that an object could derive elegance from its very usefulness and need not be overburdened with superfluous ornament. Thirdly, the enthusiasm for Japanese art was also due in part to its comparative simplicity. Finally the influence of Ruskin and that of William Morris were all important, though at the outset Morris's influence was by example rather than precept. He had been designing for many years before he wrote or spoke, publicly campaigning against the debased standards of mass production which he traced to the disappearance of honest and satisfying craftsmanship.

It is also, in some degree, to William Morris that the missionary aspect of the aesthetic movement can be traced. In one of his earliest published works, a lecture on 'The Decorative Arts' given in 1878 to the Trades Guild of Learning, Morris said 'I do not want art for a few' and likened the artist working for his own delight to the rich man eating in the presence of 'starving soldiers in a beleaguered fort'. The marked difference between this and other art movements was that it was essentially educational and 'improving' in intention. The designers and painters wished not only to work in a new way but to convince the general public of the rightness of their views. Hence one of the most influential figures of the whole movement was Oscar Wilde, who lectured and spread the views of his more creative associates. And even Whistler, who had no interest in the social aspects of art, felt it his duty as an artist to uphold good taste and impose it on others.

As part of the same process, books on the decorative arts appeared in quantities in the 1870s and '80s. Obviously they were nothing like the lush, coloured publications of the twentieth century but none the less these books were very fully illustrated and their authors were concerned to inform their readers of the standards at which they should aim in furnishing and decoration. The authors were not in complete agreement in their exact interpretation of 'art' but there was a consensus of opinion on the need for an alteration in design of all kinds.

The earliest and one of the most influential of these guides for the amateur was C. L. Eastlake's *Hints on Household Taste*, originally published as a series of articles in the *Cornhill Magazine* and first issued as a fully illustrated book in 1867. In the introduction Eastlake wrote 'half the effect of every room which is planned must ultimately depend on the manner in which it is fitted up and, if our national taste is ever to assume a definite character, let us hope that the inside of our dwellings will reflect it no less than the walls by which they are enclosed'. Other books and articles followed in profusion, some dealing with interior decoration in general, others with individual rooms such as a series which included *The Bedroom and the Boudoir* by Lady Baker (1878), *The Dining Room* by Mrs Loftie of the same year. But authors did not confine themselves to interior decoration. Mrs Haweis, a popular author, wrote on *The Art of Beauty* and concerned herself with every aspect of decoration, dress and jewellery and even considered the colour of hair which was aesthetically acceptable. Mrs Haweis had in her writing the same objective as Eastlake and others of her contemporaries though she did not think of herself as an aesthete and did not think highly of Queen Anne architecture. Similarly another influential writer and lecturer, Lucy Crane, the sister of the better-known Walter, while putting forward many aesthetic ideas, spoke scornfully of 'art embroidery, art decoration and the like tautological expressions' and suggested that they had been invented by shopkeepers to please that part of the public which was attracted by fashion and novelty.

In addition to books on every aspect of decorative art, new periodicals abounded and the old-established ones such as the *Art Journal* were re-designed in a new format with a new type of illustration often printed in soft browns and sepias, colours second only in popularity to the aesthetic green –

'No tint which common blue and yellow mingled make
But green y wrought of sepia without stint
With indigo and lake.'[6]

Two of the earliest periodicals in this field were *The Architect* and *The British Architect* first published in 1869 and 1874 respectively. Both voiced advanced opinions and were illustrated by reproductions of pen drawings instead of the tight engravings of earlier architectural publications. The only two

Victorian periodicals devoted to furniture started at the end of the 'seventies, as did *The Magazine of Art, The Journal of Decorative Art, Decoration* and *The Artist*, subtitled 'Journal of Home Culture'.

The emphasis on home culture and on amateur work of all kinds sprang naturally from the aesthetic concept of art embracing every aspect of life and several of the periodicals were as much concerned with the amateur artist and craftsman as with professional work. Another aspect of the movement was the proliferation of art groups and societies and of amateur craft workers. One of these bodies was the Home Arts and Industries Association, dedicated to 'spread knowledge of Art Handwork among the people', whose members carved woodwork and made repoussé copper vessels. The lady amateur made her appearance in the eighteen-seventies, painting panels on furniture and decorating plates and vases in addition to her traditional pursuit of embroidery. One firm of artistic tradesmen, Messrs Howell and James, organized an annual exhibition of painting on pottery at which amateurs and professionals showed their skill and prizes were awarded by a selection committee of Academicians. At the Paris International Exhibition of 1878 Howell and James actually included amateur work in their exhibit.

At this distance the eighteen-seventies and 'eighties seem to have an atmosphere quite unlike any other part of the Victorian period. Coupled with the artistic activity was a certain sense of excitement at new scientific developments that encroached on home life. Electric light, the telephone and new methods of transport produced as much copy for the cartoonist as did the Art Movement itself. *Punch* encouraged its readers to laugh at scientific jokes, which have proved eventually not fantasy but fairly accurate prophecy, and similarly though the Aesthetic Movement had its ludicrous aspects it did contain the seeds of ideas which later gained general acceptance.

Over forty years ago, when early Victorian bric-à-brac was already fashionable in some circles, Roger Fry forecast that later generations would become sentimental about the 'eighties, a period which he regarded with horror, having been brought up in an artistic home surrounded by 'black polished wood with spidery lines of conventional flowers incised in the wood and then gilt'.[7] At least one piece of furniture in this manner survives which was decorated by Roger Fry's aunt (plate 1). Writing in 1919 Fry said 'we at this moment have no inkling of the lies they (our successors) will invent about the 'eighties to amuse themselves. We only know that when the time comes the legend will have taken shape and, from that moment on, the objects of the time will have the property of emanation.' With this warning in mind and the wealth of available evidence it should be possible to establish the reality beyond the legend of the 'eighties, beyond the vision of artistic interiors in which elegant drooping figures on spindly Morris chairs gazed at their blue and white china or sketched sunflowers.

Chapter 2

RED BRICK AND SUNFLOWERS

The architectural innovation of the 'seventies and 'eighties was the introduction of an entirely new style called, somewhat inaccurately by both admirers and critics, 'Queen Anne'. It was essentially a domestic and secular style and, like other aspects of the Aesthetic Movement, was confined to England and America. While the rest of Europe continued to produce variations on the flamboyant and relatively cumbersome forms associated with the 'High Victorian' period, the English-speaking countries embarked on a revival of domestic building with some concern for comfort and convenience as well as for picturesque effect. It is to the aesthetes and their associates that we owe the red brick houses of Chelsea and Kensington, the great blocks of mansion flats embellished with terracotta sunflowers and many more modest urban dwellings each with its own garden.

Until the eighteen-seventies, though a version of Italianate classic was the accepted style for banks, club houses and the more pretentious type of town house, architecture was predominantly Gothic in one form or another. Even the reformers such as Pugin, Morris, Street or Butterfield, remained convinced Gothicists throughout their careers, believing that English architecture had gone astray at the end of the sixteenth century or even earlier when pure Gothic was abandoned and foreign influences contributed to the eclectic elaborations of Elizabethan and Jacobean building. It was felt that the national traditions of architecture had been still further damaged by the introduction of Palladian classicism and that only by turning the clock back to the days of pure medieval Gothic and by ignoring the intervening regrettable foreign-inspired developments could a truly English style be evolved. A desire for a genuine style expressing the aspirations of the nineteenth century inspired much architecture that in retrospect appears mere plagiarism. However, while the revived Gothic or 'pointed' architecture was considered appropriate for places of worship and could be applied with success to such large buildings as guildhalls, town halls and law courts, it led to curious and inconvenient results as a domestic style.

As early as 1857 in his *Remarks on Secular and Domestic Architecture* Gilbert Scott (1811–78), though advocating building based on a serious understanding of Gothic architecture, expressed the hope that 'the practice of building abbeys for gentlemen's residences is gone' and 'that the use of castles having long since gone by, people will henceforth be content to live

26 'Honeysuckle', designed by William Morris, 1876, and printed on Indian tusser silk by Thomas Wardle, Leek. *London, Victoria and Albert Museum.*

27 Part of a bedspread in indigo-dyed linen embroidered in coloured silks, designed by William Morris, 1877. *London, Victoria and Albert Museum.*

28 Detail of a curtain with *appliqué* and embroidery in crewel wools. Designed by H.R.H. Princess Louise and worked at the Royal School of Art Needlework, 1877. *Manchester, Town Hall.*

29 'Tulip' chintz, designed by William Morris, 1875. *London, Victoria and Albert Museum.*

36

29

32

in houses'. The practice, however, continued for some years longer and one of the first architects to rebel against it was J. J. Stevenson (1831–1908) who was able to take the revolutionary step of abandoning Gothic when he built a house for himself in London in 1871. Not only was the house of red brick but it was built in present-day Bayswater Road in an area of stucco houses in the classical taste. Stevenson called it the 'Red House' like another landmark in the history of domestic architecture, the William Morris house designed by Philip Webb ten years earlier. Stevenson's house was actually of brownish brick with brighter red details and mouldings and with sash windows; it was designed with some thought for comfort and convenience as well as style. Whatever the architect's intentions, he launched a fashion which by 1880 had reached such proportions that it was said that 'cheap builders are possessed by the idea that red brick, a blue pot and a fat sunflower in the window are all that is needed to be fashionably aesthetic and Queen Anne.' This comment and an account of an interview with Stevenson appeared in the periodical *The Queen* in 1880 and was later published with other descriptions of artistic houses in book form as *Beautiful Houses*. It is amusing to note that while the author, Mrs Haweis, a popular arbiter of taste, poured scorn on the Queen Anne fashion, her own little book was printed in a simulated eighteenth-century format and in pseudo-Queen Anne type face which incidentally makes it extremely difficult to read. Mrs Haweis described how 'Mr Stevenson began by following enthusiastically the Gothic Renaissance movement but transferred his affections when practical experience convinced him that Gothic architecture and decoration have many demerits when applied to modern houses, especially town houses. The waste of space, the frequent inevitable darkness which complicate the difficulties of Gothic domestic architecture when it has to be combined with nineteenth-century ideas of comfort and luxury are avoided by the adoption of the classic, of course in its more picturesque forms.' This note on the inevitability of the picturesque exactly sets the mood of the late 'seventies and 'eighties when 'picturesque' was a favourite term of commendation and a necessary attribute of any successful design.

While Stevenson's house was the first considered architectural work in the new idiom, the first of the red brick houses in London had actually been built in 1861 by the novelist Thackeray for his own occupation. A modest and relatively undistinguished house it was soon to be overshadowed, as it still is, by its larger neighbour, Number 1, Kensington Palace Green, designed in a semi-Gothic manner by Philip Webb (1831–1915). Thackeray's novel *Henry Esmond*, subtitled 'A Colonel in the Service of Her Majesty Queen Anne' had appeared a few years earlier, rapidly becoming a best seller. Thackeray clearly regarded the period as his own and it was natural that he should provide himself with a pseudo-Queen Anne setting in a house that may well have provided the name for the new style. That this literary origin of the name was accepted even by architects is proved by an article in *The British Architect* in 1875 in which William Burges wrote: 'It has been said and with great truth that the real restorer of medieval art was Sir Walter Scott – in the same way Thackeray, by means of his writing, has made Queen Anne's style popular.' Burges, whose own work was based on

30 'Tanjor Lotus', tusser silk damask, made by T. Wardle, Leek, for Liberty & Co., about 1875. *London, Victoria and Albert Museum.*

31 Panel of tiles painted in 'Persian' colours by William de Morgan about 1885. *London; Courtesy of the Trustees, Old Battersea House.*

32 Tiles, transfer printed and painted in colours, made by T. & F. G. Booth, Church Bank Pottery, Tunstall, Staffordshire, dated 1883. *In the author's possession.*

33 Earthenware tiles painted in colours, with the mark of W. B. Simpson on the reverse, 1878. *West Berlin, Kunstgewerbemuseum.*

French thirteenth-century architecture, went on to give an uncharitable but not wholly inaccurate recipe for the new style. 'To take an ordinary red brick house and to put as many gables and dormers and bow windows as possible – in fact to cut up the outlines; the great object being to get the picturesque by any and every means. The windows should be long and narrow and filled with lead glazing or with small frames divided by straight bars painted white – the ornamental parts consist of a few scrolls in the brickwork and coarse woodwork occasionally verging on the Jacobean.' The observations on narrow windows and gables came rather strangely from one who was literally still building castles as residences.

The main characteristics of the Queen Anne style can be clearly identified whether on large or small buildings. The most prominent feature, of course, was the use of red brick of all kinds. As one lyrical enthusiast put it: 'He must be strangely insensible to the charms of the picturesque who has not felt his mind refreshed and his daily load lightened by their glow of unwonted colour.' A dark red brick was usually used for the main structure, finely-jointed, smooth brickwork of a lighter, brighter red for porches, gables, mouldings and other projections and moulded terracotta for more elaborate ornament. This frequently incorporated the date of erection of the house and almost always used the sunflower as the main decorative motif. The sunflower appeared either as a repeating pattern, as in Cheniston Lodge (plate 43), or growing in an urn-like plant pot (plates 35, 37, 38). One of the earliest panels of this kind is on the gable of Norman Shaw's Lowther Lodge, built in 1874, now the Royal Geographical Society in Kensington Gore (plates 39, 40). A rare variation in decoration was the use of Japanese motifs exactly similar to those found on contemporary embroidery or silver (plates 36, 41, 42). Chimneys were very tall and ornamented with projecting vertical ribs of brickwork emphasizing the height of the building. Gables were curved and shaped or stepped in the Dutch manner producing a variation of the style which came to be known as 'Pont Street Dutch' from the area of Chelsea in which it was most prevalent. One of the most impressive houses of this 'Dutch' kind was built in Harrington Gardens, South Kensington, in 1884 for W. S. Gilbert (1836–1911), who like so many other Philistines, was much involved in the movement he lampooned.

Apart from the gables themselves, smaller gable-shaped panels were incorporated in the Queen Anne buildings and the broken pediment was a popular form, much like that used in contemporary furniture design. The other important innovation which radically changed the appearance of houses, both inside and out, was the introduction of large sash windows instead of the small windows previously dictated by the mullions of the Gothic style. These larger windows were relatively tall, adding to the vertical emphasis of the whole design, and the glass was divided into small panes by wooden glazing bars painted white. Another characteristic feature of the windows was that the upper part was further subdivided and filled with plain coloured glass or sometimes painted in grisaille. The style usually involved a quantity of external woodwork in the form of balconies, balustrades and supporting brackets and this, like the window bars, was painted white.

The same component parts were used in varied ways by a number of architects who between them produced an essentially domestic architectural form in which the façade, though consciously picturesque, reflected the interior arrangement of the building. A decorative feature which was particularly popular for smaller houses in rural settings was tile-hanging on gables and window bays. This innovation can be attributed to W. Eden Nesfield (1835–88) whose first essay in the new manner was a modest little lodge in Kew Gardens. Built in 1866, it was described at the time as an archaeological exercise in early eighteenth-century brickwork and, like most of Nesfield's work, was an entirely personal solution to the particular problem on hand. He was one of the very few architects whose work was influenced by Japanese design and the decoration of some of his buildings incorporates a frieze of stylized sunflowers or discs which Nesfield himself called his 'pies'! While Nesfield was responsible for one or two large buildings, such as Cloverley Hall in Shropshire, his main contribution was in the realm of modest buildings in the small towns and villages of southern England where his combination of original forms and traditional picturesque detail blended with the existing brick houses of the eighteenth century.

By the early eighteen-seventies the existence of the Queen Anne school of architecture was thoroughly established, whether its origins were literary or architectural. An editorial article in *The Architect* for 24 May 1873 explained that 'the name has been in vague use for three or four years past' but that with the sending of Queen Anne designs to the Royal Academy by Norman Shaw (1831–1912) and G. F. Bodley (1827–1902), both previously known for their Gothic work, the movement could be assumed to have become respectable and established. The writer then listed the 'principal leaders of the new school' including Norman Shaw, Bodley, Nesfield, Philip Webb, J. J. Stevenson, William Butterfield and others all of whom were said to have repudiated the thirteenth century for everything but ecclesiastical work. To the list was added another, unexpected name which linked Queen Anne and the Aesthetes. The unknown author referred to Dante Gabriel

Fig. 1 Drawing of a blacksmith's forge and cottage designed by W. Eden Nesfield at Cheavely Hall, Cheshire, 1881.

Rossetti as 'one more moving spirit artistic rather than architectural'. Rossetti's name was also mentioned in the following year, 1874, in a lecture given to the Royal Institute of British Architects by Stevenson himself, when he explained the new movement to his fellow architects. He asserted that the Queen Anne school was no mere fashion but a genuine style, 'the outcome of our common want picturesquely expressed'.

As it happened one of the common wants of the time was a great number of new schools and a major factor in the spread of the new style was a most unusually enlightened piece of official patronage. As a result of the Elementary Education Act of 1870 the School Board for London was established and Stevenson's partner, E. R. Robson (1836–1917), was appointed architect to the Board. There were no precedents for an elementary school architecture and after considering the problem from all angles Robson began by the selection of brick as the best and cheapest material for use in London. He decided also that, even had it been convenient, Gothic with its ecclesiastical associations would be inappropriate for school architecture at a period when education had begun to be recognized as a secular and non-sectarian responsibility. Starting from the simple brick style of the late seventeenth and early eighteenth century, many modest examples of which were still extant in most of the older London boroughs, Robson evolved the type of Board School with which Londoners are still familiar today. These schools were consciously intended to form the nucleus of a good modern style expressive of the second half of the nineteenth century. They were tall buildings with large windows, Queen Anne detail and the same vertical emphasis found in artistic red brick houses, and each varied according to the requirements of the site. Like the houses each school had its panel of decorative terracotta and was surmounted by white painted ornamental woodwork or ironwork. Two hundred and sixty such schools were built in London between 1870 and 1881.

Clearly this was too much work for one architect but Robson did retain responsibility for the overall design policy as well as designing himself many of the buildings, such as that in Wornington Road in North Kensington (plate 65). In an article characteristically called 'Art as Applied to Town Schools' Robson explained his missionary approach to school building and related it to the Aesthetic Movement as a whole. 'It must always be among the high purposes for which Art exists to make any home brighter and more interesting, nobler if you will. We have seen how abject are the homes of countless thousands. If we can make the homes of these poor persons brighter, more interesting, nobler, by so treating the necessary Board Schools planted in their midst as to make each building undertake a sort of leavening influence, we have set on foot a permanent and ever active good – this is no mere theory – it is already proved by the manner in which builders of ordinary houses are imitating the Board Schools in every direction.' It seems unlikely that the homes of the poor were actually made brighter by these 'picturesque temples called Board Schools' but they did dominate the London townscape, as they still do in some areas, and the speculative builders produced terraces of red brick houses in the same idiom. Even the more drab tenement buildings were sometimes decorated, as an afterthought, by a single sunflower as a modest conciliatory gesture to Art and Queen Anne (plate 34).

Bedford Park today looks, to the casual passer-by, much like any other residential area of West London but on closer inspection it is apparent that all the houses are similar in character and in date and some, those with extra large windows, suggest that they may well have been intended as homes for artists. In fact this was the first garden suburb, the Utopian home for aesthetes, which set the pattern for the main English contribution to late nineteenth-century architecture, the detached house in its own garden. While others concerned themselves with improving the living conditions of artisans, Mr Jonathan T. Carr (1845–1915), a property speculator with artistic inclinations, decided to build a village which would provide ideal living conditions for the professional classes. He purchased a hundred acres of well-established garden and orchard land, close to the Thames and served by a railway from the City but considered far enough out to avoid the fogs of London. Between 1876 and 1881 he built there 'a little red town made up of the quaintest Queen Anne houses' employing as his architects E. W. Godwin and Norman Shaw.

Picturesque houses had previously been the prerogative of the rich since any deviation from the conventional, even in interior decoration, had been too expensive for the average householder. Carr decided that if sufficient numbers wanted interesting houses and artistic decoration it should be possible for his architects to produce varied results from materials sufficiently alike to be bought in large quantities. Thus the picturesque could be made accessible, if not actually cheap. So on roads curved or straight, according to taste, and all lined with blossoming trees were built three hundred and fifty red brick houses, all slightly different and all engaged in 'pleasing competition as to which could be the prettiest' (plate 55).
To quote a contemporary verse:

'Thus was a village builded
For all who are aesthete
Whose precious soul it fill did
With utter joy complete.'

This is part of the 'Ballad of Bedford Park' published in *St James's Gazette* in 1881 and one of the many both flippant and serious poetic efforts inspired by the project.

In the manner of later garden cities, Carr provided other amenities for the artistic tenants of his picturesque houses. There was a village store, an inn or tavern, a club house and a church which was one of the few attempts at the use of the new style for a place of worship. Everything was consistently Queen Anne and quaintly old-fashioned with interior decoration in keeping with the red brick architecture. It seems likely that Carr was responsible not only for the first garden suburb but indirectly for many an 'olde worlde' teashop and inn influenced by his personal vision of Old England.

The first eighteen houses were actually completed in 1876 from designs by E. W. Godwin (1837–86) whose published work had suggested to Carr that he was one of the only architects practising at the time who was capable of combining artistic detail, practical design and economy. One of the first families to occupy a Bedford Park artistic home was that of the poet W. B. Yeats who, in later life, described the initial wonder of living in a house 'like those we had seen in pictures and even [meeting] people dressed like people in story books'. It is recorded elsewhere that the inhabitants of Bedford Park, whether artists or members of the professional classes, were inclined to affect aesthetic dress and on occasion actually wore eighteenth-century costume. Another observer, the artist Edwin Austin Abbey, said that Bedford Park 'made him feel like walking through a watercolour sketch'.

There were a number of criticisms of Godwin's designs on practical rather than aesthetic grounds and after a somewhat acrimonious exchange of views in the professional press architect and client parted. In 1877 Norman Shaw was engaged as the main architect for the project. He or his associates designed the remainder of the houses as well as the public buildings. The overall effect of the Tabard Inn and its adjoining buildings still suggests the seventeenth century not least because Shaw ignored the new development of plate glass windows and equipped his store with large bays divided into small panes of glass. The inn sign outside was painted by an artist resident in one of the nearby houses and internally the inn was decorated with tiles designed by William de Morgan and Walter Crane in glowing colours said to be 'all of Early English and most pronounced Aesthetic type'. This comment throws interesting light on the misleading character of contemporary description. The surviving tiles at the Tabard Inn are essentially of their times, the design of the de Morgan ones being built on the typical structural form of a William Morris wallpaper design and totally unrelated to 'Early English' design of the Queen Anne period or any other date. The birds and flowers echo the gardens of the surrounding houses as do de Morgan's sunflower tiles of a similar date (plate 31). Socially the most important building of the community was the Club which differed from others of its date in catering for both ladies and gentlemen. It had a domestic atmosphere with flowers in all the rooms, china and glass ornaments about the place and 'the prettiest of all possible ladies' drawing rooms'. Apart from the more usual amenities of billiards, cards and games rooms, the Club had a library in which the newest books were available and accommodation for the concerts, dramatic performances and fancy dress parties which were an essential part of the community's life. From the beginning a high proportion of the residents were practising artists and the Art School, the interior of which seems to have had a slightly discordant Moorish flavour, was one of the centres of the life of Bedford Park. The students, reported to be 'of decidedly aesthetic type both as to mode of dress and fashion of arranging their hair', worked at all the usual art school subjects as well as the more specialized ones of art needlework, art pottery and art tile painting.

In architectural spheres, the aesthetic approach did not preclude the consideration of practical details. It was in a Bedford Park house that one of the first air-conditioning systems in England was installed and the whole project was advertised as having not only artistic but sanitary advantages over any other housing development. This example seems to have been followed elsewhere, as for instance in Eastbourne where in 1881 a combined 'Aesthetic Fine Art and Sanitary Exhibition' was held, with public lectures on both subjects. The whole Bedford Park scheme embodied the aesthetic concept of art embracing all aspects of life. The resident artists shared the social life of the businessmen who travelled daily from the City; all lived in honest brick houses, uncamouflaged by a covering of conventional stucco, in which paint was not used to imitate marble or grained woodwork; and almost everyone chose to live with Japanese prints and William Morris wallpapers. The purchasers and lessees of the houses were able to choose their own decorations but there seems to have been such unanimity of view on the virtues of green or terracotta paintwork and Morris papers that at one time it was suggested that a branch of Morris and Company could with profit be set up at Bedford Park. After a remarkably successful start the project proved either impractical or unprofitable as a business venture and the original company was dissolved, but much of its character has survived as a unique and practical demonstration of the aims of the Aesthetic Movement.

Around 1880, American enthusiasm grew to such an extent that, inspired by the example of Bedford Park, it was proposed to build not a mere village but an 'aesthetic city'. The project, however, did not materialize. One writer in the English press suggested that 'we are convinced that the harmless enthusiasts who at present imagine themselves enamoured of existence in a town inhabited by none but aesthetes will, before they have paid their second quarter's rates, be ready to rush from the place as if it were stricken by the plague.'

Examples of Queen Anne architecture can still be found all over London where it was particularly favoured by prosperous artists. There are 'quaint red mansions' in such areas as Melbury Road, Kensington, where Lord Leighton's house was at the centre of a colony of artists. E. W. Godwin built numbers of red brick houses and studios in Tite Street, Chelsea (plate 63), in addition to Whistler's famous 'White House' (plate 64). This was recently demolished but the others, with their large studio windows and restrained terracotta ornament, survive (plate 62). Godwin became a specialist in studio architecture and in 1878 built one in the grounds of Kensington Palace for Princess Louise, Queen Victoria's sculptress daughter. The largest concentration of artists' houses was in the Hampstead area and of these a fairly considerable number were designed by Norman Shaw, for instance 39 Frognal built for Kate Greenaway in 1885. Outside London red brick Queen Anne is, aptly enough, principally associated with art schools and other educational buildings.

Queen Anne or the picturesque classic did not prove the answer to the problem of an English national style but for a decade or so it did produce some pleasant and fresh domestic architecture based loosely on the vernacular of the eighteenth century. In the latter part of the century red brick architecture was adopted for larger domestic buildings, such as blocks of mansion flats, and the style degenerated into heaviness and pomposity overburdened with elaborate terracotta ornament.

Chapter 3

THE AESTHETIC INTERIOR

The adjective 'Victorian' as applied to English furniture and decoration still conjures up for most people a vision of over-elaborate, over-furnished interiors filled with carved mahogany sideboards, plush curtains, turkey carpets and papiermâché. As far as can be judged from the surviving evidence and from first-hand descriptions, this is a fair picture of furnishing by the prosperous in the first part of Queen Victoria's reign and of the style which continued until the end of the century in many middle-class homes. For different reasons both the furnishing trade and the buying public were conservative in their tastes and understandably preoccupied with increasing domestic comfort. In considering style there is a tendency to forget the social changes embraced by the Victorian period which made it possible for manufacturers in the latter part of the nineteenth century to compete in selling ornamental domestic paraphernalia of all kinds to the humbler householders whose early Victorian forebears had only rudimentary furniture and had eaten from wooden trenchers or pewter plates. Stylistically the term 'Victorian' covers everything from the simple classic forms of the late Regency to the curves and fantasies of the Quaint or Art Nouveau.

In the late eighteen-sixties and early 'seventies a new style of interior decoration arrived with the Aesthetic Movement and was given the name 'art' to indicate that its exponents were opposed to the crude commercial colours and vulgar display of High Victorian decoration. The name was also proof of the division which had arisen in the middle of the century between art and manufacture. In the eighteenth century a well-made chair or table was accepted as an artistic object within the obvious limitations of its kind. With the coming of the new mass-producing manufacturing industries came the new idea that art had to be added after the mere maker had done his job. This conception applied to all forms of household equipment but particularly to furniture. Whereas, before the industrial revolution, there had been furniture of varying quality made by either urban or rural craftsmen, in the latter part of the nineteenth century there were three quite separate categories. These were commercially made furniture, art furniture, and pieces made by rural craftsmen; both the latter categories were assumed to be necessarily superior to the former.

The term 'art' furniture seems traceable, like so many other names of the period, to C. L. Eastlake's *Hints on Household Taste* first published in England

34 Victoria Dwellings,
Clerkenwell Road, London.
Detail of brickwork, 1882.

35 Sunflowers in terracotta,
Fitzjohn's Avenue, London,
about 1878.

36 Detail of the decoration of
Barclay's Bank, Saffron Walden,
designed by W. Eden Nesfield,
1874.

35

34   36

Overleaf

37 Central façade of Carlisle
Mansions, Cheyne Walk, London,
1886.

38 Another detail from the
central façade of Carlisle
Mansions, Cheyne Walk, London,
1886.

39

39 North-facing façade of
Lowther Lodge, designed by
Norman Shaw, 1874; now the
Royal Geographical Society,
Kensington Gore, London.

40 Part of north-facing façade of
Lowther Lodge, showing in detail
the sunflower motif in the gable.

Overleaf

41 Panel in the façade of
Carlisle Mansions, Cheyne Walk,
1886.

42 Another panel in the façade of
Carlisle Mansions, Cheyne Walk,
1886.

in 1867. Its influence can be appreciated from the fact that there were four English editions and six published in the United States. The title 'art' furniture was not in general use until the mid 'seventies but the first 'Art Furniture Company' was established in 1867. Obviously a little before its time, it was reported to be failing a year later because, although its products were well designed, they were too expensive and not appreciated. Even before the publication of his book Eastlake associated art with craft and regarded both as the opposite of fashion and commerce which he held to be the joint villains of the contemporary scene. He complained of the quality of the design of industrially produced furniture and suggested that simplicity could only be achieved by individually designed pieces specially made by rural craftsmen. 'We have at the present time no more artistic workman in his way than the country cartwright. His system of construction is always sound and such little decoration as he is enabled to introduce seems appropriate because it is in accordance with the traditional development and necessary forms.'[1] This passage contains in brief all Eastlake's novel recommendations for good design. Furniture and other domestic equipment should be simple and soundly constructed, the decoration should be minimal and the whole design should be based on function or purpose. 'Every article of manufacture should indicate by its general design the purpose to which it will be applied.'[2] The theme of simplicity runs through all Eastlake's written work. It is a little difficult to reconcile the illustrations in *Hints on Household Taste* with the text but this is a problem with so much nineteenth-century design in all media. New principles were applied by designers to existing forms as they were known and the interiors or individual pieces of furniture chosen to illustrate these principles were interpreted by contemporary artists or draughtsmen in the manner fashionable at the time. The resulting drawings look Victorian to a modern eye while the text is often remarkably in accord with twentieth-century ideas of design.

In America the influence of Eastlake's book was such that a form of restrained Gothic furniture, still known as 'Eastlake style', was made there (plate 6). In fact C. L. Eastlake (1836–1906), though an architect by training, was not a practising designer. He was involved in a variety of activities and ultimately became Keeper of the National Gallery in London. His book contains some designs attributed to him but the text reveals that they were individually created pieces for his personal use and presumably made by his country cartwright. The contemporary American author, Mrs Harriett Prescott Spofford, writing in 1878, recorded that the popularity of the book produced a demand for Eastlake style furniture.[3] As such furniture did not exist the New York upholsterers, book in hand, were compelled to devise some. Mrs Spofford continued, 'The Eastlake style is from solid wood unvarnished and usually without veneer, made in the simplest manner that conforms to the purpose of the article, with plain uprights and transverses slightly chamfered at the corners.' Popular as this furniture may have become in some circles it was not universally admired in the United States. A writer in *The Cincinatti Trade List* of 1874 condemned the leading New York houses for their folly in adopting English Gothic styles after designs by Eastlake and hoped that the regrettable fashion would not extend to their

43　Cheniston Lodge, Marlowes Road, Kensington, 1885. Typical 'Queen Anne' town house with sunflower decoration in the brickwork.

city. While some people saw Eastlake in the forefront of an advanced movement the Cincinatti writer took the opposite view. 'Of all the clumsy, ugly inventions, or rather copies, the sort advocated by Eastlake deserves most to be condemned. There may be some use of medievalising household articles in England where this movement is but parallel to the reassertion of conservatism as proclaimed by the recent parliamentary elections – but whereas in our country comfort and beauty are the only guides, the manifest incongruity and unsuitableness of the fashion give it but small chance of being extensively adopted.'

While these views may have seemed convincing from the other side of the Atlantic, in England, the home of the Aesthetic Movement, it would have been impossible to find in contemporary life the political equivalent of the many styles covered by the general term 'art' decoration. Furniture alone ranged in name, if not in form, over almost every English and European historic style. Art furniture illustrated in such periodicals as *The Cabinet Maker* and *The Furniture Gazette* appeared with the labels 'Tudor', 'Jacobean', 'Anglo-Japanese', 'Italian Renaissance' or 'Queen Anne' and one of the fashionable cabinet-making firms of the day was described as a pioneer of the 'Backward-Ho' movement. 'Queen Anne' was the most popular label but this covered almost anything, as one writer defined it, that possessed 'remarkable simplicity and quietness of old work together with great picturesqueness and quaintness.'[4] However diverse their approach almost all designers were actually aiming at 'an avowed Victorian or New English style which need not be ashamed to acknowledge itself as such'[5] and all furniture of the period has a common recognizable flavour.

The fashionable woods were black or ebonized baywood, basswood or black walnut. These replaced the long popular, highly polished mahogany and dark Danzig oak. Bright, almost orange, mahogany and satinwood had a certain vogue around 1880 and oak seems to have been acceptable if light in colour and often even unpolished. Other light woods used for chairs, such as the many variations on the rush-bottom chair made popular by William Morris (plate 20), were stained green, dark blue or black. The fashion for ebonized furniture, which lasted about fifteen years, was introduced when Collinson and Lock showed their first ebonized cabinet in 1871 at the International Exhibition held in London (plate 54). Designed and produced with painted decoration of semi-classical languid ladies, it was regarded as an artistic novelty which started a fashion; ten years later, in 1881, ebonized cabinets 'were legion and so like each other that none can claim any special merit over the others.'[6] The original design was remade and exhibited in Europe and America and one version, with decoration designed by Burne-Jones, was bought by Prince Johannes Liechtenstein. The legs, supports, balusters and other uprights of art furniture were slender and turned, characteristics that create an air of comparative instability, and this led to much of the simple fun made of the aesthetic home (plate 67). Carving was confined to formal, repeating designs in thin incised lines, often gilt, to give emphasis in the black wood (plate 1). The accepted method of decoration of more elaborate pieces was painting which completely replaced the rich carving of the High Victorian period (plate 52). 'One good painted panel

A door in the Drawing-room

a bit of the finger plate

Fig. 2 Drawing of a painted door in the drawing-room of the home of an architect.

is worth ten thousand times more than all the meretricious carving with which so much of our modern furniture is filled'.[7] From the painting of panels on furniture the idea spread to the painting of actual interiors; vases of flowers and other artistic subjects were often painted on door panels (plate 49). Another popular form of decoration was the carving of little balustrades, echoing the turned decoration of legs and other structural members, round the tops of cabinet furniture and round the edges of shelves (plate 1). While most art furniture design was rectilinear, one curved feature survived and is characteristic of the period: this was the overhanging support of the upper parts of cabinets and sideboards (plates 3, 53), a shape which also appeared in overmantels and sometimes as the frieze around a complete room.

The keynote of aesthetic interior decoration was the use of subdued or even dull colours, particularly a range of dull greens, and the comparatively lightweight furniture was usually set against wallpaper in these tones by one of the accepted designers, such as William Morris, Bruce J. Talbert or Lewis F. Day. The use of secondary or tertiary colours was the aesthetic reaction to the bright, harsh colours favoured in the middle of the century. Technical advances had made possible a new range of colours which were considered by artistic critics, with some justice, to be 'hideous through their extreme purity'[8] and most writers on interior decoration particularly warned their readers against the use of white for either walls or ceilings. On the other hand some enthusiasts went rather too far in the other direction and many light and fresh wallpaper designs, notably those of Lewis F. Day and Bruce J. Talbert (plates 9, 10, 11), were sold most successfully in dreary versions printed in shades of dull green and khaki. William Morris advised against the use of pure colour but also said 'on the other hand do not fall into the trap of a dingy bilious yellow-green, a colour for which I have a special hatred because I have been supposed to have somewhat brought it into vogue. I assure you I am not really responsible for it.' One aspect of the aesthetic interior for which Morris was almost certainly responsible was the use of painted woodwork and this often in a dark green. The first important interior decoration projects undertaken by Morris and Company in about 1866 were the Armoury at St James's Palace and the Green Dining-Room at the Victoria and Albert Museum. Both these rooms had dark painted woodwork and a dull green predominated in the decorative schemes. While the rooms in St James's Palace were obviously comparatively unknown, the Green Dining-Room was in daily use by architects, designers and art students of all kinds, and one architect at the heart of the aesthetic movement, E. W. Godwin, is known to have derived his ideas for painted woodwork from that room. The colour of the woodwork was an important feature of the average room as it was customary at this date to divide walls horizontally in at least three parts often separated by bands of wood moulding. Whereas today most interior walls would be covered by a single paper or colour the aesthetic practice, which became generally accepted in late Victorian times, was to divide a wall into a dado some three feet high surmounted by a wooden moulding which protected the wall from chairs and other furniture, a filling for the main upper wall, and a frieze (see plates 12,

13). Between the filling and the frieze there was either a picture rail or, more often, a narrow shelf on which porcelain or other bric-à-brac could be shown (plate 51). This led to a series of patterned wallpapers being used in association with each other (plates 12, 13) and occasionally to the use of the same paper, such as Morris's well-known 'Pomegranate', in three different colourways in the same room (plate 58). Another result of this wall division was the production, for use on staircases, of curiously angled papers, designed to fit the treads of the stairs and the sloping dado.

The word dado had long been in use as an architectural term but it seems to have entered the domestic vocabulary in the mid eighteen-seventies and for some reason it became one of the key words of the aesthetic fashion, its mere mention providing a source of merriment for the Philistines. Another innovation for wall covering at this date was the use of Indian matting and Japanese leather paper, both first imported into England in the mid eighteen-seventies. The fine matting was used for covering the lower wall or dado and was also recommended for floors. Its soft golden colour provided a pleasantly warm background for lightweight furniture. The imitation leather paper, slightly embossed and gilt, was hung on the main wall or on the frieze and it provided a rich background for blue and white china or Japanese lacquer trays. This type of paper was also pasted on furniture, being a cheaper and more durable alternative to painted panels (plate 2).

Broadly speaking it can be said that the aesthetic interior contained less furniture and far fewer ornaments than had been customary in the middle of the century. Heavily carved furniture, large mirrors in gilt frames, white ceilings and bright colours were regarded as vulgar, while shades of soft green, blue and white porcelain, Japanese fans and peacock feathers, and William Morris wallpaper were the marks of an enlightened home. However there was considerable variation within these broad outlines and it is of some interest to read some contemporary descriptions of actual rooms or methods of decoration recommended by arbiters of taste who wrote handy guide books for amateurs or articles in professional papers.

An article in *The Furniture Gazette* of 1875 typically entitled 'The Moral Influence of Decoration' gives a detailed description of a recently-decorated pretty house. In the dining-room 'the walls are a dark drab with a high dado of mauve and drab in alternate bands and a frieze of sober hued stamped leather . . . the furniture shows sufficient variety to avoid monotony while harmony is yet preserved throughout . . . over the fireplace is a mantelpiece of oak and walnut with ebonised mouldings . . . a curtain that divides the dining room from the small ante chamber or reception room beyond. This curtain which is the work of the lady of the house is a quite perfect work of art. In colour it is a dark, bluish green, and it is crossed by broad bands of pale yellow and black velvet beneath which are embroidered at intervals circular devices of peacock's feathers. These, with the rare blue china, Salviatti vases, the choice brass work and bronzes and other *objets d'art* sprinkled about serve as points of positive colour to brighten the room.' Mrs Haweis, in her little handbook *The Art of Beauty*, provided a general rather than a specific recipe for room decoration also based on a mixture of colour. 'Doors should be tall and should match in effect, if not in colour, the walls and ceiling – that is a room with a deep blue ceiling and walls of Vandyck brown and similar dark colours may have doors black or deep sage green; a room whose walls and ceiling are chiefly coloured with tertiary citrine (a mixture of orange and green, a yellowish colour) may have doors of a very dull green or brownish purple; a room papered with scarlet deeply indented to break the monotony of that tint may have black or sage green doors and wainscott.' It is easy to see from this last fashionable description with its air of authority how *Punch* came to define the aesthetic interior as one on which dust was allowed to accumulate so that colours should be suitably subdued.

In contrast to these popular ideas of art decoration the real aesthetic interiors devised by the architect E. W. Godwin and J. McNeil Whistler (1834–1903) must have been of astonishing elegance and simplicity. Whistler's work as an interior decorator, apart from the famous Peacock Room (plate 59), was principally in devising settings for his own pictures when they were exhibited. On one occasion the gallery was decorated in shades of brown, on another in white and yellow with the chairs painted yellow and even the door attendant dressed in a white and yellow livery. One of his subtlest colour schemes was for an exhibition 'Notes, Harmonies, Nocturnes' held in 1884, when he decorated the gallery with delicate rose-coloured walls, a white dado, white chairs and pale azaleas in rose flushed jars. Such decoration could be regarded as pure showmanship, but Godwin on the other hand was responsible for the decoration of numbers of domestic interiors and descriptions of some of these survive though the houses have gone.

When clients permitted it, Godwin designed not only the house and the furniture but chose the wallpapers, often of his own design, supervised the mixing of the paint and finally selected pictures and ornaments. In 1874 he decorated a conventional London terrace house for his own occupation. The entrance hall and all the ground floor rooms were uncarpeted and the bare floorboards were oiled and waxed. The dado was of Indian matting and the upper part of the wall covered with a paper in a conventional pattern in umber and vellum colour. The ceiling was also pale, creamy vellum colour and all the paintwork a light red. In a series of articles published in *The Architect* in 1876 Godwin gave detailed descriptions of every room, even to his exact recipe for the mixing of the paint. In the drawing-room he used 'a rather dark-toned yellow of which yellow ochre is the base, but combined with white, sprinkled with gamboge, Prussian blue and vermilion' and so on through each room. The overall effect was so unusual that it was recorded by various contemporaries, such as the actor Forbes-Robertson who remembered that 'the floor was covered with straw-coloured matting and there was a dado of the same material. Above the dado were white walls and the hangings were of cretonne with a fine Japanese pattern in delicate grey-blue. The chairs were of wicker with cushions like the hangings.'[9] According to the designer there were also a few Japanese fans against the skirting and on the ceiling, some Japanese vases and a few light-weight pieces of furniture. 'No description, however, except perhaps that which may be conveyed in the form of music, can give an idea of the tenderness and, if I may say so, the ultra refinement of the delicate tones of colour which form the background to the few but unquestionable gems in this exquisitely sensitive room.'[10]

These few words contain the essence of the aesthetic approach to design or 'Art Work' as Godwin called it, with the implied interrelationship of the arts and everyday life. None but an aesthete would have contemplated the description of his London drawing-room in terms of music. But while they provided the material for artistic settings, all the designers of the day were not aesthetes.

One of the most prolific and influential designers was Bruce J. Talbert (1838–81) who seems to have been an essentially practical man though a sensitive draughtsman with positive views on design. A professional industrial designer, trained as an architect in his native Scotland, Talbert's first move south was to Manchester where he began to design for the cabinet-making firm of Doveston Bird and Hull in 1862. He quickly established a reputation as one of the leading furniture designers in the simplified Gothic manner which was then fashionable. In 1867 he had published a book of designs, *Gothic Forms Applied to Furniture*, which contained details of individual pieces and suggestions for complete rooms as well as a preface in which Talbert explained his approach to design which was similar to that of Eastlake. The same authoritarian note was struck in Talbert's writing on design as in that of most of his contemporaries. Readers were not offered suggestions but firmly told what was right and proper for each room of their house. As far as is known, Talbert was only designing furniture and metalwork at this date but he advised on all aspects of decoration and even took into consideration current fashion, suggesting that adequate contrast to horizontals and verticals would be supplied by 'the ever-changing curves' of those for whom rooms were designed.

Based on a sound practical knowledge of materials and structural principles, his furniture was relatively simple for its date and incorporated geometric designs in inlay, a little low-relief carving and sometimes small enamels (plates 7, 8). This was Talbert's alternative to the more popular painted panels which he regarded as impractical unless the paintings were inset in such a way as to avoid constant rubbing in use. Small enamel panels of birds and animals introduced a pleasant colour note into his designs. Talbert worked for a number of leading cabinet-makers but his book and a later publication, *Examples of Ancient and Modern Furniture*, were so widely studied that by the mid-'seventies a casual observer would have imagined that he had a hand in far more than he could possibly have actually designed. A fellow designer and chronicler of style development, J. Moyr Smith (working 1870–89), writing soon after Talbert's death, attributed the beginning of public interest in 'art furniture' to a single plate in *Gothic Forms*. This was a design for a drawing-room which, with its curved frieze, sunflower decorations and comparative spaciousness, may well have been ahead of its time, but it is difficult to see in it the seeds of revolution.

Talbert's wallpaper and textile designs, however, are as attractive to modern eyes as they must have been when they were first produced. As he worked anonymously for a number of firms it is not possible to be certain of the extent of Talbert's work but enough has been identified to realize the freshness and originality of his flat pattern design (plates 70, 71). His characteristic style, much imitated after his early death, involved the use of sharply-delineated flowers, fruit and leaves, all without shading, arranged formally on a ground ornament often derived from a Japanese source. His surviving drawings show that, though the final effect was somewhat stylized, his work was based on a detailed observation of natural forms. Talbert's most popular papers were the 'Sunflower' series exhibited at the Paris Universal Exhibition of 1878. In addition to the conventional printed papers these included designs for embossed leather and flocks in the usual dull green colour (plate 9). These designs were awarded a Gold Medal and were much illustrated and imitated. During the late 'seventies and early 'eighties Talbert-type sunflowers appeared on woven and printed fabrics of all kinds and were particularly popular in stamped velvet or plush. Talbert's own designs for printed textiles actually predate the better known ones of William Morris.

Morris did not design for textiles until the early 1870s and the actual fabrics were first marketed about 1875 after a period of experiment with dyes in which he joined forces with a dyer and printer from Leek in Staffordshire, Thomas Wardle. Together they revived the lost art of indigo dyeing and attempted, with the use of vegetable dyes, to achieve the 'repose of tint' found in native printed Indian fabrics as opposed to the vivid colours current in Europe. These fabrics printed with native dyes had recently been rediscovered and proved, once more in practical form, the aesthetic contention of the superiority of craft processes over commercial products. The desired result was achieved by printing Morris's designs in soft subdued colours on the newly discovered tusser silk, hand-woven in India (plate 26). A collection of these fabrics, together with others commissioned by Liberty and Co., was also shown at Paris in 1878. Morris's prime influence on the aesthetic home, however, was through the medium of his wallpapers which, unlike the fabrics, were amongst the earliest productions of Morris and Company. Almost all designed by Morris himself and printed by the principal art wallpaper firm, Jeffrey and Company, these papers were an immediate success. The 'Daisy', dating from 1862, was the first Morris wallpaper and, with its formal, almost stiff, treatment of the simplest of flowers in flat colours, it was the complete antithesis of the lush two-dimensional papers in the French style then popular with the trade. The other contribution of the Morris firm was their lightweight rush seated chair, which was based on a traditional Sussex country type. It could be bought for only a few shillings and thus was well within the reach of the most modest aspiring aesthete.

Lewis F. Day (1845–1910) was an artist and a prolific writer on design subjects and, like Talbert, some of his most attractive designs were for wallpapers (plates 10, 11). Day entered the art world by way of a firm of glass painters where he was employed as a clerk. He moved to another firm where he graduated to actual glass design, a subject in which he retained a critical interest all his life. In 1870 he started his own business and produced designs for wallpapers, pottery, glass, textiles, furniture and virtually everything for the artistic home. In the latter part of the century he exerted considerable influence in various official capacities; he was art director of a textile firm, a Master of the Art Workers' Guild and an examiner for the Royal Society of Arts, but in the aesthetic period it was by his own work that he influenced public taste. His flat, pattern designs for wallpapers and textiles were usually based on a strictly geometric diaper form but the end product has a remarkable freedom and flow of line in which it is possible to see the seeds of Art Nouveau, a development which Day lived to see and deplore. It is no doubt the sinuous and flowing line which has made subsequent reprints of his textiles so popular. In all his flat patterns Day was particularly successful in disguising the repeats so that a geometrically-based design could appear to be an apparently random arrangement of daisies or apple blossom. Much of his work was based on the ubiquitous sunflower and his most original contribution to the aesthetic home was a series of designs for mantelpiece clocks in which the sunflower was used as the dial. These were all designed for the firm of Howell and James, whose work is described in Chapter VII. These attractive little clocks, many of which can still be found today, contain in miniature all the elements of the larger pieces of art furniture. The cases are usually of ebonized wood with simple turned or incised ornament and surmounted by galleries and turned terminal knobs. The clock faces are of ceramic tiles painted in blue and white in a variety of charming designs with the sunflower as the central feature (plates 44, 45). Lewis Day's furniture design was confined to relatively large exhibition pieces, aesthetic only in their use of painted panels.

Art furniture of considerable charm was produced by numbers of lesser figures few of whose names are known. One of the best of these was H. W. Batley (working 1873–93) who produced a handsome volume of etchings recording his own work[11] (plate 53). The plates were drawn and etched by the designer and some of them illustrated actual schemes of decoration while others were works of imagination, such as the room of 1872 in which Batley described his aim of adapting Egyptian ornament to modern use. The book typifies the aesthetic search for some practical basis for a new Victorian style. The plates were printed in artistic sepia, the text was in a Gothic typeface and there are traces of Egyptian, Jacobean and Japanese influence in the designs themselves, as well as a very personal treatment of plant form almost suggesting the first stirrings of Art Nouveau. On the evidence of surviving pieces of furniture, Batley hardly did himself justice in his etchings. A piano in the Victoria and Albert Museum, originally shown at the Paris Exhibition of 1878, is a modest and attractive piece of furniture in bright mahogany with low relief carving based on Japanese motifs (plate 17). Its comparative simplicity and restraint make it easy to see why English art furniture made such an impact on the Continent where heavy, dark carved pieces were still the order of the day.

Art furniture and decoration were also designed by some architects whose eminence in their own profession has tended to overshadow their domestic work. Norman Shaw in his Queen Anne period was associated with the London joinery firm of W. H. Lascelles for whom he designed a range of lightweight furniture stained blue or deep red and decorated with panels

44   Clock in ebonized wood with incised decoration and painted porcelain face, probably designed by Lewis F. Day, 1880. *London, Victoria and Albert Museum.*

45   Clock in ebonized wood with painted tile face and brass panels, designed by Lewis F. Day and made by Howell & James about 1878. *Private collection.*

46   Firescreen made in mahogany, inset with tiles, made by W. B. Simpson & Sons, about 1880. *Walthamstow, William Morris Gallery.*

47 Bureau from the Edwin Gould
Bedroom at Lyndhurst, Tarrytown,
New York, in bird's eye maple, with
inset tiles in the Japanese style;
American, about 1870. Note the
image of the wardrobe in the mirror.
*National Trust for Historic
Preservation, U.S.A.*

48 Bed from the Edwin Gould
Bedroom at Lyndhurst, New York.
*National Trust for Historic
Preservation, U.S.A.*

49 Dining-room door at
18 Stafford Terrace, designed and
painted by Linley Sambourne,
1874. *The Countess of Rosse.*

48

50 Hanging cupboard and
painted wall panels from The
Grove, Harborne, Birmingham,
designed by J. H. Chamberlain,
1877; from a contemporary
photograph.

51 Billiards room, designed by
Thomas Jeckyll, 1870; from a
contemporary photograph.

52 Cabinet in ebonized wood
with painted panels and turned and
fret decoration; probably made by
Collinson & Lock about 1875.
David Verey Esq.

50

51

53

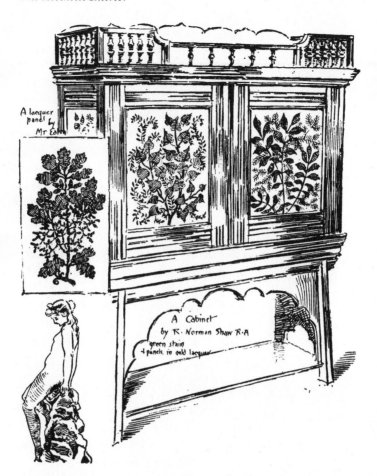

Fig. 3 Drawing of a cabinet designed by R. Norman Shaw and shown at the Furniture Exhibition, 1882.

53 Design for a drawing-room mantelpiece in satinwood, inlaid and carved, the backing panelled in silk. Exhibited at the Paris Exhibition, 1878. Plate 6 from *A Series of Studies for Domestic Furniture and Decoration* designed and etched by H. W. Batley, 1883.

painted in colours and gilt. These pieces were exhibited from 1875 until the mid eighteen-eighties in a gallery run jointly with the Royal School of Needlework in that centre of all art work, South Kensington. Contemporary opinion seems to have been divided on the quality of this furniture but there appeared to be no doubt about the virtues of the design, each article appearing what it really was, 'neither the usefulness nor the ornamentation clashing with each other'. In 1877, despite his growing architectural practice, Shaw became a partner in the firm of Aldam Heaton whose work included embroidery, stained glass, carpets, wallpaper, embossed leather-work and furniture all designed in Shaw's office. J. Aldam Heaton had previously been responsible for some of the painted decoration of Shaw's furniture. The trend of furniture designing towards the end of the century is indicated by the fact that the later pieces produced by this partnership were often faithful reproductions of actual Chippendale and Hepplewhite.

None of Shaw's art furniture is known to have survived but pieces by another eminent architect, Alfred Waterhouse (1830–1905), exist today. Waterhouse, by no means an aesthete but certainly a leader of fashion, was responsible for some interesting interior decoration conforming to aesthetic standards and for some original furniture design. One of his most complete schemes of decoration was that for Blackmoor House in Hampshire built for the Earl of Selborne and completed in 1872. Externally the house is

77

slightly Gothic and a little forbidding but a wrought iron sunflower sur-mounting one of the gables gives a clue to the interior. The rooms were all oak panelled to dado height and covered with Japanese leather paper or stencilled decoration above. Art tiles with figure subjects were used in each of the individually-designed fireplaces but it was in the furniture that the architect showed his skill and originality. The larger pieces (plate 3), like the house itself, have slight Gothic echoes but the smaller pieces, notably the chairs, were completely original in design and carried out in practice East-lake's theories. In light oak or ebonized wood, upholstered in natural leather, these chairs owed nothing to any traditional forms and yet they exploited the best of traditional craftsmanship (plate 4).

By the mid 'eighties the Aesthetic Movement was spent but it left a permanent mark on interior decoration. Even the most conservative critics of the Movement admitted that the long-term effects on design were benefi-cial in correcting the excesses of the High Victorian period. The statement that 'it would be difficult now for anyone buying furniture and domestic utensils of any sort to avoid becoming possessed of a considerable number of objects which were really good in form and colour' appeared in *The Spectator* in 1881,[12] and was echoed by other writers. The more extreme products of the Art Movement died a natural death, speeded by impractica-bility, but the best survived and passed into general use. Two new furniture styles had been added to the designer's repertory: so-called Queen Anne settled into a neo-Georgian vein, generally accepted for drawing-rooms well into the twentieth century, and the simple rustic style, typified by Morris chairs, unexpectedly provided the basis for the Quaint or English Art Nouveau. Some of the earliest essays in this style were drawing-room chairs, made north of London in High Wycombe, based directly on old craft traditions. But probably the most important legacy of the Art Movement was the concept of fitness for purpose which led eventually to the functional design of the twentieth century.

Chapter 4

THE JAPANESE
TASTE

The impact of Japan on the decorative arts in England in the second half of the nineteenth century has never been fully explained though the influence itself passed through three clear phases each of which conveniently falls into a decade. In the eighteen-sixties it was a matter for individual collectors and enthusiasts, both in England and in France, and in this period Whistler produced his earliest Japanese-inspired paintings, Rossetti designed a Japanese bookbinding and a few amateurs began to collect lacquer, porcelain, glass and prints. In the 'seventies, the fashion was in full swing amongst informed people and Japanism and the Aesthetic Movement were virtually synonymous, while the Philistines scoffed. Interior decoration and furniture design were based on what were believed to be Japanese principles, rather than on the superficial forms and ornament which were the hallmark of the 'eighties when what had been a movement became a mania. Every mantelpiece in every enlightened household bore at least one Japanese fan, parasols were used as summer firescreens, popular magazines and ball programmes were printed in asymmetrical semi-Japanese style and asymmetry of form and ornament spread to pottery, porcelain, silver and furniture. To the great British public – as one writer explained in the trade periodical *The Cabinet Maker and Art Furnisher* – 'Japanese art has taught the advantages of asymmetrical arrangements so that one need not always have pairs'. By the 'nineties the fashion for anglicized Japanism had gone and Japanese art, together with other characteristics of the Aesthetic Movement, had become one of the contributory elements in Art Nouveau.

It has long been assumed that Japanese objects were first seen in London and Paris in about 1860, mainly on the basis of varied apocryphal stories of pots wrapped in superb Japanese prints which were treasured by their finders. These discoveries were followed by the exhibition of the arts of Japan at the International Exhibition in London in 1862 when the first British Minister in Japan, Sir Rutherford Alcock, showed his personal collection of lacquer, bronze and porcelain. This exhibit certainly made a considerable impact on the informed visitor as an art of relative simplicity and restraint in the midst of High Victorian elaborations but it was really not the beginning of the story. Even during the centuries when Japan was cut off from the rest of the world, there had been a trickle of trade through the Dutch and Chinese who had limited trading rights at Nagasaki. As a

79

result of this, when the Department of Practical Art, the forerunner of the present Victoria and Albert Museum, was established in London in 1852, two thirds of its tiny collection in Class V, 'Furniture and Upholstery etc.', were either japanned or papiermâché and nearly all were directly ascribed to Japan or China. These pieces were small and not of the highest quality and presumably the only people influenced by them in 1852 were the makers of fashionable papiermâché who traditionally imitated Chinese lacquer-work of earlier centuries. Two years later in 1854 a complete exhibition of Japanese applied art was held in London in the gallery of the Old Water Colour Society in Pall Mall East, from which the Science and Art Department made fairly extensive purchases on the recommendation of those eminent critics, Messrs Richard Redgrave and Henry Cole. Though this seems to have been the first large display of Japanese wares in London it would appear to have made little mark and in contemporary press comment there was no suggestion that the exhibition was an event of any significance. Clearly the mood of the times was not receptive to this new art form.

The exhibition may well have been one of the results of the first expedition to Japan made in July 1853 by the American Commodore Perry. From then until 1858, when both the British and the Americans achieved a limited commercial treaty with Japan, there was intermittent contact with the country and indeed representatives of the British navy and some civilians were continuously resident in Yedo for six months in 1857, becoming fairly well acquainted with life and art. A charming little book *Japanese Fragments* was written in 1860 by Captain Sherard Osborn, one of the English officers on this expedition. It is fuller than the title suggests, providing a general history of Japanese relations with Europe and an account of everyday life and arts and is illustrated by facsimile reproductions of Japanese colour woodcuts of landscape subjects. The book did not appear until 1861 since Captain Osborn had difficulty in finding a printer of sufficient skill for this work. He finally settled for Bradbury and Evans, the printers of the illustrated periodical *Once a Week*.

This period of negotiation in Japan no doubt explains the Hokusai prints seen by Whistler in Paris in 1856 and a series of roller-printed cottons with designs lifted direct from Japanese prints which were produced and marketed by Daniel Lee of Manchester in 1858, fully four years before the normally accepted date for the introduction of Japanese goods into England. Obviously some Japanese goods were known in Europe in the sixteenth and seventeenth centuries but the figures on these chintzes were taken directly from wood block prints of a type not produced until the middle of the eighteenth century when Japan was firmly closed to foreigners. In other respects these are typical Victorian furnishing prints but the usual floral wreaths happen to contain Japanese figures rather than some picturesque rustic or rural scene.

One of the curious things about the whole Japanese mania is that it seems to have been sparked off, not by long-haired aesthetes who were the products of the movement rather than initiators, but by a staunch devotee of medievalism. This was the architect William Burges, amongst whose private papers are preserved some of the first Japanese prints to be collected in England and all dating from the 1850s. These include some of the usual single figure prints and several sheets of rather crudely executed popular prints of children's games, badges and figures of Europeans, as well as book wrappers, one of which is a repeating pattern of what came to be Whistler's butterfly. The combination in Burges of an enthusiasm for thirteenth-century France and nineteenth-century Japan, so superficially curious, is easily explained. It was not primarily the form of Gothic architecture which appealed to Burges but a romanticized view of the conditions which produced it, and so it was with Japanese art. 'To any student of our reviving arts of the thirteenth century', wrote Burges of the 1862 International Exhibition, 'an hour or even a day or two spent in the Japanese Department will by no means be lost time, for these hitherto unknown barbarians appear not only to know all that the middle ages knew but in some respects are beyond them and us as well'. Here, Burges felt, was perfect medieval art. He was particularly impressed by the success of the audacious asymmetrical ornament, or the Japanese 'horror of regularity' as he called it, and by the beauty of their patterned papers.

After the South Kensington Exhibition of 1862, some of the exhibits were disposed of by Messrs Farmer and Rogers in the Oriental Department of their Great Cloak & Shawl Emporium, of which young Mr Lasenby Liberty, subsequently the founder of Liberty's, became manager in the following year. Another large consignment of Japanese goods was sold by public auction having arrived too late to be exhibited.

Arthur Lasenby Liberty (1843–1917) was Oriental Manager for Farmer and Rogers for twelve years and on 17 May 1875 he opened his own small shop at 218a Regent Street. The timing of the venture seems to have been exactly right for, with an increasing demand for Oriental art amongst a small and informed public, the venture was so successful that within twelve months he was able to extend, first to the adjoining premises and later into another shop at 120 Regent Street. His own knowledge and taste was based on experience of the best and highest quality goods as they came into the country during the first years of contact with Japan and before increasing public demand led to the inevitable vulgarization, and the whole project was based on Liberty's personal enthusiasm for the goods he sold and a genuine desire to improve public taste.

The customers in the first years of trading included William Morris, Carlyle, Ruskin, the Rossettis, Burne-Jones, Whistler, the architects Norman Shaw and E. W. Godwin and numbers of other figures associated with the arts. The initial enthusiasm for the venture can be assessed from some of the contemporary press accounts. Godwin writing in *The Architect* of 23 December 1876, only eighteen months after the opening, describes the excitement when it was rumoured that a new importation of Japanese fans was expected and 'that certain cases of them would be opened in a certain little shop near the top of Regent Street'. The waiting crowd agog for the opening included, apart from 'a bevy of ladies', three distinguished painters with their wives, a distinguished traveller, a well-known baronet and 'two architects of well-known names'. On this occasion unfortunately the waiting crowd was disappointed as the cases were delayed until the evening but this left the author free to explore the shop, from ground floor to attics, which were 'literally crammed with objects of oriental manufacture'. These included carpets, matting, embroideries, small pieces of bamboo and lacquered furniture, porcelain, bronzes, dress fabrics and curios of all kinds and even 'Tokio Tooth Powder', to the beneficial properties of which the maidens of Japan owed the pearly whiteness of their teeth. Already in Liberty's first catalogue of 'Eastern Art Manufactures' there are objects described as Anglo-Japanese and clearly specifically made for the European market and Godwin confessed with misgiving that a certain coarseness was creeping into some Japanese work. 'The fans of ten years ago are for the most part lovely in delicate colour and exquisite in drawing, but the great majority of the fans of today that have come under my observation, are impregnated with the crudeness of the European's sense of colour, and are immeasurably beneath the older examples in both qualities mentioned.' Clearly the mania of the 'eighties for cheap and tawdry bric-à-brac was already on its way. On the whole, however, Liberty continued to maintain the high standards he had set himself not only in Japanese goods but also in those from other parts of the Orient. Silks and dress fabrics were imported from Persia, China and India, as well as from Japan, and such care was taken over design that the Indian silks were produced especially for Liberty only after consultation with the authorities at the newly-established Indian Museum. Only a year after the shop opened Liberty were selling Indian silks, woven to their own specifications and printed in England with vegetable dyes 'in artistic, aesthetic and useful colours', in the same way as some of William Morris's designs.

Other Japanese warehouses were set up in various parts of London, notably a distinguished and short-lived venture in Farringdon Street in the City started in 1879 by Dr Christopher Dresser who had the unique distinction amongst English designers of the day of having visited Japan. Other smaller oriental departments were opened in some of the new large stores, such as William Whiteley's, Swan and Edgar and Debenham's but these, like Liberty's fabrics, were more concerned with fashionable costume than with Japanese *objets d'art*. It is to Liberty's that the main credit must go for maintaining the flow of high-quality Japanese blue and white porcelain, bronzes and lacquer objects, collected by the followers of the Aesthetic Movement in the 'seventies, as well as the cheap fans and toys which filled every mantelpiece in the 'eighties.

It seems likely that the original collectors of Japanese objects, having no shop to turn to, acquired them from the post-exhibition sale in 1862. This may well have been the source of William Burges's prints and leather paper, Dante Gabriel Rossetti's porcelain and screens, and where the architect E. W. Godwin bought the colour prints with which, in the same year, he decorated his Bristol home, reputedly the first house in England to be decorated according to Japanese-inspired principles. It is curious that Godwin's name and work are so little known and he is remembered mainly as the father of Gordon and Edith Craig. In fact he was an original architect, a prolific architectural journalist, an authority on various aspects of Gothic building, a designer of theatrical productions, furniture, wallpaper, textiles and almost every aspect of interior decoration and, in a large measure, was responsible for the Victorian enthusiasm for things Japanese. In addition he was something of a personal publicist and he was generally regarded by his contemporaries as one of the leaders of the Aesthetic Movement, together with his friends Whistler and the young Oscar Wilde.

In his early days as a conventional church architect Godwin had designed some stained glass and embroidery but his first large furniture commission was for the Guildhall at Northampton. The building was designed in 1861 but by the time the furniture was ordered he had come under the influence of Japanese art. Consequently the Gothic building was equipped with original, simple furniture owing almost nothing to contemporary furniture design. Godwin's next major work was Dromore Castle in County Limerick where one of the aesthete's trademarks, the peacock, taken directly from a Japanese crest, made its first appearance in Godwin's work. All the furniture, of simple rectilinear structure, was made in 1867 to the designer's specifications in oiled wainscot oak, the material a concession to the Gothic building, or ebonized mahogany, his favourite furniture wood. From the early 'sixties onwards, or from the time of his first contact with William Burges, Godwin devoted as much time to the study of Japanese art and its principles as he had in the previous ten years to the medieval. It was not his exclusive study, however, as his notebooks are filled with drawings from a variety of historic sources and from nature itself. This eclectic approach, which produced Japanese ornament in an Irish castle, is explained by Godwin's advice to students that they should study all that they could and take what good they could from every country and age but work in no particular style. If asked what style their work was – a reasonable Victorian enquiry – they should say: 'It is my own.' This is certainly true of all Godwin's furniture designs and such pieces as have survived. His most characteristic pieces were usually described as Anglo-Japanese but in their elegant simplicity they have little or nothing in common with the rickety imitation bamboo of the 'trade' productions of the latter part of the century.

From 1867, when he made his first furniture designs, until his death twenty years later Godwin designed considerable quantities of furniture, much of it, such as the well known elegant coffee table or the ebonized sideboard (plates 24, 2), originally for his own use and subsequently put into production. The sideboard, like the contemporary pieces for Dromore Castle, is a perfect example of Godwin's declared aim of basing his designs on the grouping of solid and void without additional ornament. The only ornaments he allowed himself were panels of Japanese leather paper, as in this case, or the occasional use of panels of actual Japanese carving, both commodities available at the time from Liberty's.

Possibly the most influential of Godwin's furniture was the group designed for the Paris Exhibition of 1878. This seems to have been the occasion on which real and pseudo-Japanese design came into its own. Not only were there actual Japanese exhibits, but such an august building as the official English Pavilion erected for the use of the Prince of Wales contained a morning room of 'exceptionally modern character' with Anglo-Japanese furniture, stained glass windows (plate 120) and an embroidered frieze of

Japanese motifs made by the Ladies' Work Society. Godwin's furniture was decorated on this occasion by James McNeil Whistler. The two men had first met in about 1863 when both had already been infected with an enthusiasm for Japanese prints and they were in close touch for the rest of Godwin's life. The most famous piece of work with which their names were jointly associated was Whistler's own house in Tite Street, Chelsea, designed by Godwin in 1877 (plate 64). On the occasion of the Paris Exhibition the next year Godwin did not use his favourite ebonized mahogany and instead of the usual black the whole exhibit was in shades of yellow described by the designers as a harmony in yellow and gold. A combination of the work of an architect and a painter in this form was most unusual though it was a logical extension of their mutual study of Japanese interior design. Early Morris and Company furniture existed, which was merely a vehicle for a series of pictures, but here for the first time were purely decorative abstract paintings which were intended to complement the furniture design. The group included elegant lightweight chairs, occasional tables, a sofa, a case for music and 'The Butterfly Cabinet'. It has been suggested that it was ultimately intended for Whistler's own use but unfortunately none of the pieces seems to have survived. However, there are various contemporary descriptions of the group, some wholly admiring and some like that by the writer in the *Society of Arts Reports* who admired Godwin's Japanese-type furniture but had distinct reservations about the glaring yellows ranging from citron and sage to orange and gold.

This variation on a single colour, using only plain painted surfaces, was one of Godwin's particular enthusiasms and his usual method of work for individual clients. In 1884, when the general practice was to mix a variety of positive designs and sombre colours in one room, he designed a subtle room for Oscar Wilde in shades of white. It is easy to see why painting was an expensive form of decoration, as compared with the more usual wallpaper, when Godwin's instructions for the decorators were: 'The whole of the wood-work to be painted in enamel white and grey to a height of five feet six inches. The rest of the walls to be finished in lime white with a slight addition of black to give a greyish tone.' All these subtle gradations of pale, clear colour were inspired by Japanese colour prints.

In another room designed for himself in 1872 when he was living with the actress Ellen Terry, Godwin based the entire décor on the pineapple. For example the woodwork was 'painted the pale green sometimes seen at the stem of a pineapple leaf when the other end has faded' which seems an instruction of extraordinary subtlety to give to the average housepainter. Another of his rooms was decorated in shades of blue and 'almost entirely furnished with Japanese things', a statement supported by his own house-hold inventory in the 'seventies and by Ellen Terry's memoirs in which she records the exceptional upbringing of the children, whose nursery walls were lined with Japanese prints, who wore tiny kimonos which made them look as Japanese as all that surrounded them and who, as a suitable treat, were taken to see an itinerant band of Japanese conjurors.

While his furniture was, as Godwin wrote himself, 'more or less founded on Japanese principles' (plate 56) his flat pattern designs, whether for wall-

54 Cabinet in ebonized wood with painted panels designed by T. E. Collcutt and made by Collinson & Lock, 1871. *London, Victoria and Albert Museum.*

55 'Tower House and Queen Anne's Grove' from a set of lithographs of Bedford Park published in 1882. *London, Victoria and Albert Museum.*

56 Watercolour sketch for a 'Japanese' cabinet, by E. W. Godwin, 1876. *London, Victoria and Albert Museum.*

57 Sketch design for a Town Hall in the 'Queen Anne' style, by E. W. Godwin, about 1876. *London, Victoria and Albert Museum.*

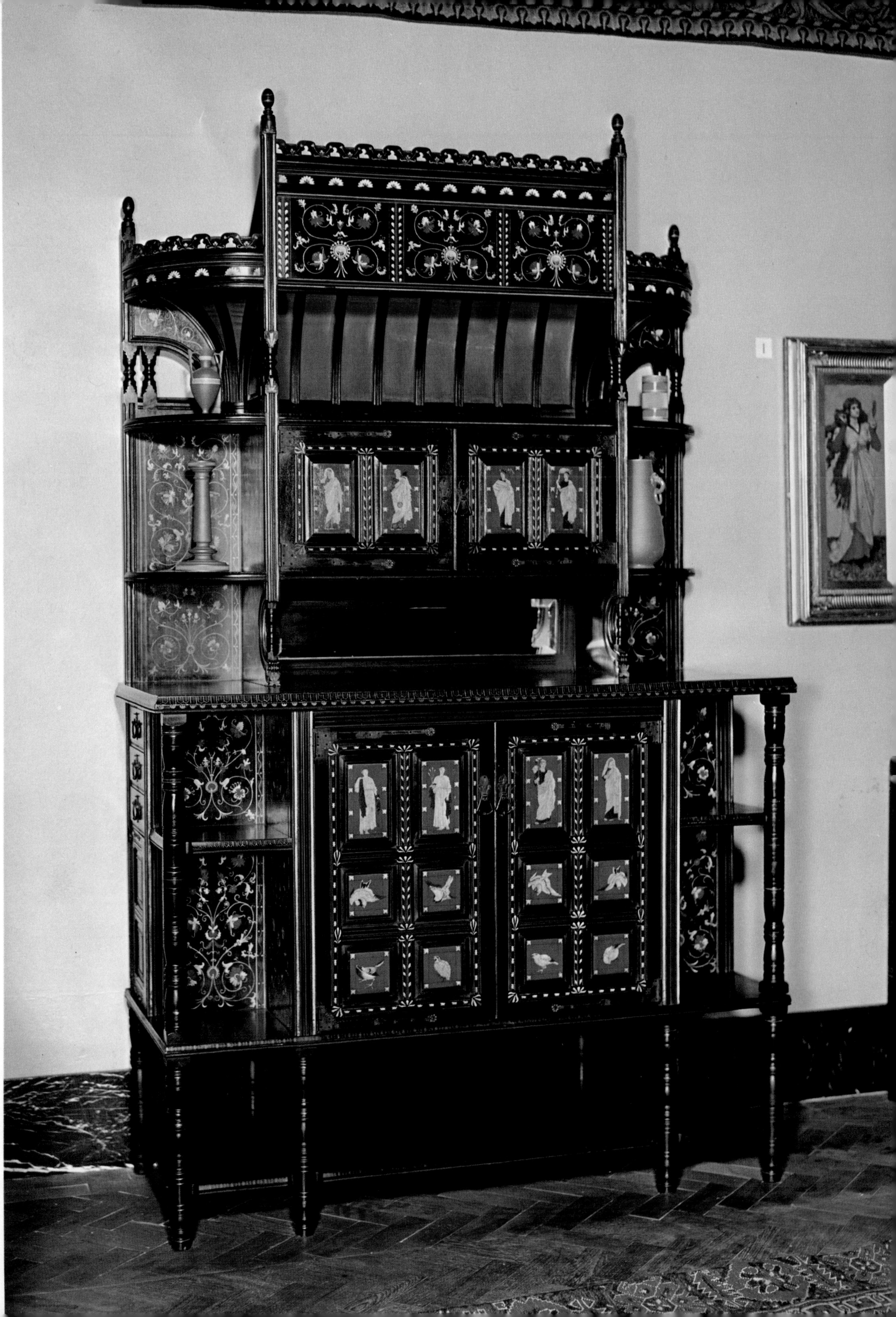

55

56

57

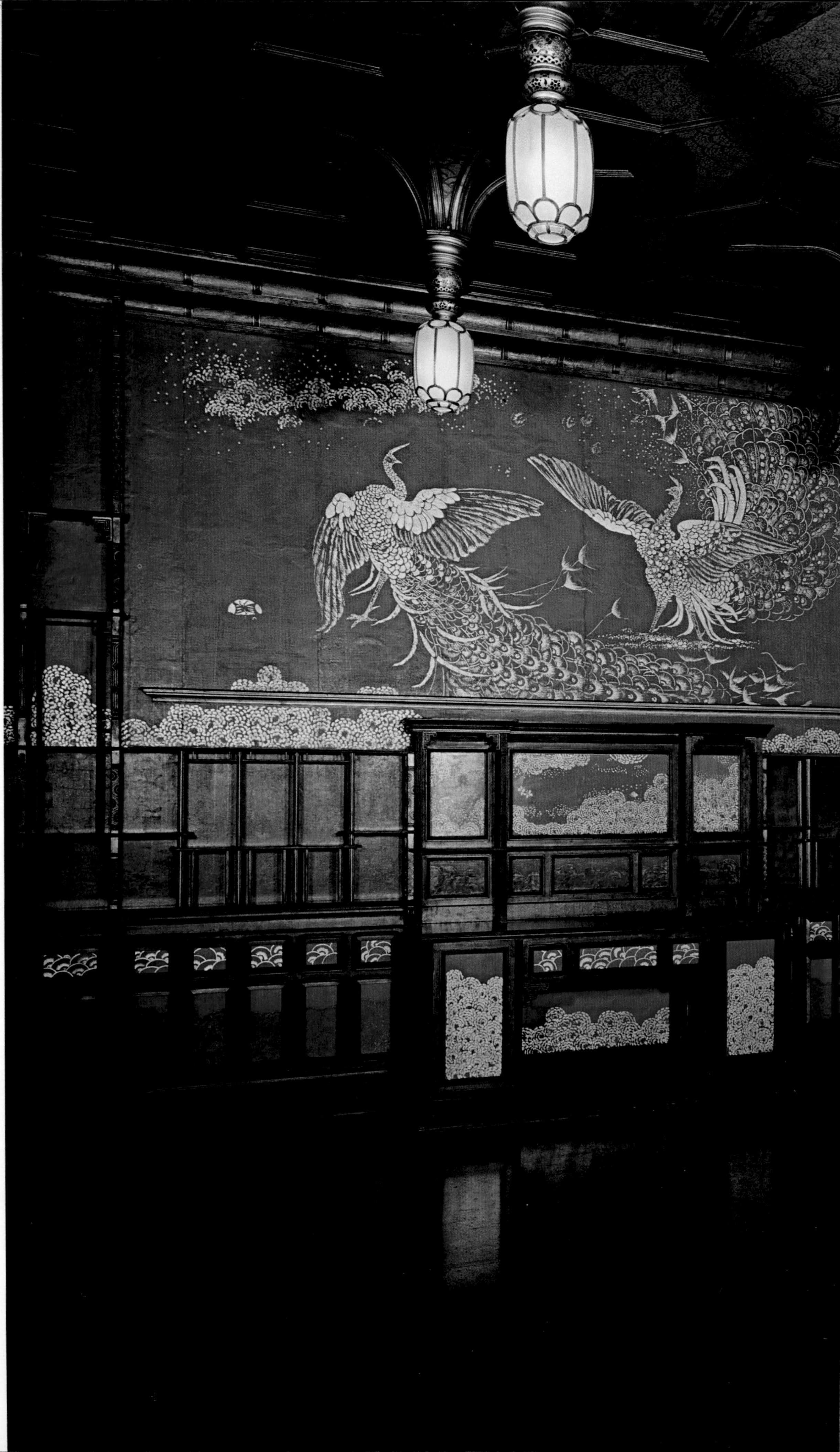

papers, tiles or textiles, were usually lifted directly or elaborated from Japanese sources. A page in one of his sketchbooks covered with detailed drawings of Japanese badges provided the motifs for several of his wallpaper and tile designs as well as obvious inspiration for textiles, such as the silks woven by Messrs Warners to Godwin's designs in about 1874 with names such as 'Nagasaki' (plate 75). This latter silk is a fairly complex design with angular linear ornament on the leaves and the ground 'full of detail but quiet', a subordination which Godwin found and admired in Japanese pattern design. The wallpapers were more diverse in character, ranging from those like the stylized 'Peacock' (plate 73) to the almost random asymmetrical designs such as the 'Bamboo' filling (plate 16), for use with the 'Peacock', and the 'Sparrow and Bamboo', all produced in the same year, 1872. This last paper, which Godwin intended to be printed in pale blue and pale green on a white ground, was usually sold in shades of the gloomy paper-stainer's green which was the hall mark of cultured taste in the 'seventies and was described by Godwin as an artistic mistake, ruining as it did the effect of his light, fresh designs as well as those of other Japanese enthusiasts like B. J. Talbert. The full range of Japanese wallpapers designed by Godwin has not yet been identified but the number can be appreciated from the fact that in 1872, when he was arranging the interior decoration of one of his larger houses, the builder's specifications enumerated at least a dozen rooms including the hall and stairs to be papered 'in different patterns at different prices all papers to be had of Messrs Jeffrey and to be Mr Godwin's patterns'.

Another 'Japanese' designer of the 'seventies was Thomas Jeckyll (1827–81) who, like Godwin, began his professional life as a Gothic architect and who had a considerable quantity of church building and restoration to his credit before he first came into contact with Japanese art and decoration. In Jeckyll's case this happened, not in London, but at another International Exhibition, that held in Paris in 1867. Architecture was singularly untouched by Japanism throughout the whole Aesthetic Movement. There was a certain asymmetry of fenestration, the deliberate use of undecorated surfaces and some rather superficially applied ornament but it was on interior decoration and furniture that the mark was made and thus after his conversion from the Gothic it was to domestic work that Jeckyll's energies were directed. His first important commission in 1870 was for a new wing of a house at 1 Holland Park for that enlightened patron and collector, Alexander Ionides. The house already included decoration by Morris and Company and Walter Crane quite apart from the owner's collections of painting and objects of virtue. Jeckyll designed a sitting-room, a billiards room, a bedroom and a servants' hall, all in the Anglo-Japanese manner, and was responsible for most of the furniture. This was much more closely related to actual oriental furniture than the designs of some of his contemporaries, both in detail and form, though obviously adapted to European use. The most distinctive feature of the sitting-room was an elaborate but elegant overmantel into the framework of which were set pieces of carved coral-coloured lacquer as a background for a collection of porcelain. The blue and white pieces were housed with style and elegance if

58   The dining-room at 18 Stafford Terrace, Kensington. The wallpaper 'Fruit and Pomegranate' by William Morris was new in 1874, the year in which the house was decorated. The sideboard was painted by Linley Sambourne. *The Countess of Rosse.*

59   The Peacock Room. Designed by Thomas Jeckyll and painted by J. M. Whistler for F. R. Leyland, 1877. *Washington, Freer Gallery.*

60   'Blossoms' by Albert Moore, 1881. Oil on canvas. *London, Courtesy of the Trustees of the Tate Gallery.*

61   'The Pelican'; pastel by Edward Burne-Jones, 1881. *Walthamstow, William Morris Gallery.*

somewhat impractically, on shelves running from floor to ceiling set against yellow walls, in the servants' hall. Judging from surviving illustrations and descriptions, however, the most successful and consistently Japanese room in the Ionides house was the billiards room (plate 51). The ceiling and walls were covered by a system of oak framing, related in proportion to the mullions and transoms of the windows. Within this framework, the cornice, dado and ceiling were made of lacquered Japanese trays and the openings in the walls were set with colour prints and paintings on silk, all of bird and flower subjects.

It was presumably as a result of this successful scheme of decoration that Jeckyll was commissioned by F. R. Leyland in 1876 to decorate his dining-room and to make it a suitable setting both for his collection of porcelain and for Whistler's 'Princesse de la Paye du Porcelain'. Overpainted with blue and gold peacocks by Whistler, it is often forgotten that Jeckyll was the designer of this remarkably original room (plate 59). In form it is a skilful blending of elements from a variety of sources. The fan-vaulted ceiling was almost a direct reproduction of the Tudor ceiling of the Watching Chamber in Hampton Court Palace with light fittings replacing the original pendant finials; the walls were lined with Spanish leather as a backing to the delicate shelving, with a strong vertical emphasis in their arrangement to counteract the restricting effect of their practical horizontal line. The only truly Japanese motif was that of the sunflower firedogs of wrought iron (plate 114). It was in the design of ironwork that Thomas Jeckyll excelled and it was the material in which he produced his most delicate and highly-wrought Japanese designs.

Soon after his conversion to the Japanese vogue, Jeckyll was employed by Barnard, Bishop and Barnard of Norwich to design for them a great cast-iron pavilion to be shown at the Philadelphia Centennial Exhibition of 1876. Transported back across the Atlantic it appeared two years later at the Paris Exhibition where it was admired both as a technical *tour de force* proving the skill of the manufacturer and as a perfect example of the application of Japanese design to contemporary use. An extraordinary structure, the pavilion was intended by the manufacturers for use upon a lawn or in ornamental grounds and it ultimately came to rest in a public park in Norwich, the town of its manufacture (plate 66). This two-tiered structure was supported on a series of cast-iron columns, with brackets and roof panels also of cast-iron, enriched with elaborate designs in low relief of birds and foliage, all of Japanese inspiration. The railing of the upper floor was of wrought iron of a fairly severe Japanese fret design but the most successful part of the whole structure was the surrounding railing, each unit of which was the aesthetic symbol, the sunflower, described at the time as 'one of the boldest and at the same time the most successful examples of modern wrought-iron work'. The treatment of both the foliage and the flower itself showed an intimate knowledge of the natural form of the plant and of the resources of the craftsman, as did the individual designs for the supporting brackets. The original drawings have a remarkable sensitivity of feeling and are some of the most attractive products of the Japanese vogue (plates 115, 116). The pavilion itself was merely an exhibition piece but the individual components were adapted by Jeckyll for use in stoves and firegrates and were in production for many years, finding their way into many an aesthetic interior, as did the sunflower in its adapted form as a firedog. The most popular of Jeckyll's cast-iron designs was that for a stove front consisting of a series of decorated circles, each containing a formalized flower and set on a ground of Japanese key diaper pattern, and he also designed cast-iron seats ornamented with Japanese cloud forms for use on railway stations in East Anglia.

Probably the most attractive form of Japanese design and one that was well within the reach of the general public was that for pottery and porcelain. Spectacular exhibition and display pieces were made by a number of manufacturers, notably the Worcester Royal Porcelain Company, but around 1880 almost every maker of table wares registered a 'Japanese' design with the Patent Office. The keynote of all these designs was an asymmetrical arrangement of fans, birds, sunflowers and almost anything remotely oriental, within the framework of the circular plate.

Another feature of this type of design was the practice of running a band of design obliquely across a circular plate or the cutting up of the whole pattern area by such bands meeting at acute angles. Occasionally the printed decoration included a European figure or landscape subject but always set in a fan or box shape placed off centre in the design indicating the oriental sympathies of the designer. One of the earliest complete services was called 'Sparrow and Bamboo' and was first made by Wedgwood in 1879. Except that the body was of Wedgwood's usual cream earthenware, the service was quite unlike their normal production (plate 83). Jugs and other vessels were straight-sided and angular and the decoration was a combination of relief moulding and transfer printing. The bamboo of the title was used as the motif for the handles of the various jugs and cups and the surface decoration was of fans moulded in relief and with a printed fan superimposed in relief only. In between the fans were sparrows and a type of kingfisher perched on boughs of plum blossom. While many designs of this kind on pottery were merely self-consciously asymmetrical and different from the conventional production, some of the more restrained examples are most attractive with painted or moulded decoration of a very high quality. Possibly the most successful were relief-decorated stoneware jugs made by such firms as W. Brownfield and Pinder, Bourne who, keeping up with fashion in this form of popular art, substituted for their usual narrative or commemorative subjects, storks or plum blossom applied seemingly at random (plates 85, 86). Some makers occasionally made objects in direct imitation of oriental forms, such as the attractive little angular teapot made by the Worcester Royal Porcelain Works in 1877 (plate 78).

The Japanese mania reached the silver trade in the mid-'seventies though in a comparatively restrained form. No attempt was made to imitate actual Japanese metal forms in original design, though one firm, Hukin and Heath of Sheffield, supplemented the real pieces of metalwork available to collectors by producing reproductions of actual Japanese and Persian metalwork by the electrotype process. As far as domestic silver was concerned the fashion took the form of the production of straight-sided or very

95

simply curved vessels decorated with engraved designs of natural plant and bird forms derived from Japanese sources (plate 90). The only elaborations of form were in handles which, like the pottery jugs, were often based on growing bamboo. A later development of the eighteen-eighties in both domestic silver and jewellery was the use of applied gilt fans or birds on the main engraved silver ground in imitation of Japanese damascened metalwork (plate 89). Some of the pieces of relatively cheap jewellery of this kind were among the most attractive products of the fashion, possibly because of their comparatively small scale.

It seems curious that in a period of outward show and opulent display, an art which was opposed in every way to these ideas should have been popular, but the reasons for the existence of the Japanese taste seem to have been as diverse as its varied manifestations. It was the elements of understatement and restraint that appealed to Godwin, Whistler and the Aesthetic Movement, and this was explained in high-flown terms by Oscar Wilde in one of his lectures. 'Only a few have learned the secret of those high hours when thought is not. The secret of the influence of Japanese art here in the West is that it has kept true to its primary and poetical conditions and has not laid upon it the burden of its own intellectual doubts, the spiritual tragedy of its sorrows.'

On the other hand, Burges and his medieval followers admired Japanese ornament for the conditions which they believed produced it and without any real understanding of purpose or aim they opened up a rich new source of design motifs for trade. With the architect's enthusiasm for light colours and elegance on the one hand and for Japanese-derived ornament on the other, plus the great flood of Japanese goods reaching Europe after the Japanese revolution of 1868, the mania knew no limits. The Japanese made their contribution to the Queen Anne interior just as surely as they did to asymmetrical magazine layouts. There were provincial exhibitions of Japanese art, Japanese balls, a Japanese village set up briefly in Knightsbridge, Japanese furniture, Japanese books and, of course, Gilbert and Sullivan's opera *The Mikado*.

By 1878 a writer in the *Society of Arts Journal* explained that 'there has been such a rage for Japanese design of late that we are tolerably well acquainted with it. From the highest to the lowest, from the Worcester Royal Porcelain Works to Parisian children's fans we have had imitations of Japanese style.' Directly or indirectly Japan was the strongest external design influence in England from the mid-'sixties until the end of the century.

Chapter 5

OSCAR WILDE AND AMERICA

The most notorious figure of the eighteen-eighties was Oscar Wilde (1854–1900) who became in his early twenties the butt of most of the fun poked at aesthetes and was lampooned as one of the central figures in Gilbert and Sullivan's *Patience*. This notoriety was remarkable in that Wilde was not the originator of any of the ideas then current; though he did claim some responsibility for initiating an artistic movement he designed nothing, painted no pictures and his creative work at the time was confined to some rather weak poetry and an early play apparently never actually staged as it was unacceptable to the Lord Chamberlain, not for aesthetic excesses but because of its democratic or left-wing sentiments. Wilde's poetry was somewhat overpraised by a small group of the more intense aesthetes probably as much for its presentation as for its literary merit. The paper, the printing and above all the binding were most considered and as one reviewer of 'Poems' of 1881 wrote 'the cover is consummate, the paper is distinctly precious, the binding beautiful and the type is utterly too'.[1]

Wilde was a most effective apostle of aestheticism, writing and lecturing on all aspects of the decorative arts and on dress reform with such zeal that, while the more serious aspects of the Art Movement are forgotten, the mention of the eighteen-eighties conjures up an image of Wilde, lily in hand, attired in a velvet knickerbocker suit. This picture is unfair to his contribution to the movement though it does seem possible that he was responsible in some degree for the choice of the aesthetic symbols of the sunflower, the lily and the peacock feather symbolizing respectively constancy, purity and beauty. The origins of the adoption of these signs or badges of right-thinking are very obscure. As early as 1882 Walter Hamilton wrote 'why the sunflower, lily and peacock's feather have become identified with the movement is not easy to explain . . . in this minor matter I believe the example of Mr Oscar Wilde has had a considerable influence'. Again this is a question of publicity rather than an original idea. In one of his published lectures Wilde said, 'You have heard, I think, a few of you, of the two flowers connected with the aesthetic movement in England and said (I assure you erroneously) to be the food of some aesthetic young men. Well let me tell you the reason we love the lily and the sunflower . . . It is because these two lovely flowers are in England the two most perfect models of design, the most naturally adapted for decorative art – the gaudy leonine beauty of the one and the precious liveliness of the other giving to the artist the most entire and perfect joy.'[2] In fact the use of both the sunflower, 'that bright emblem of constancy', and the peacock feather originate from the study of Japanese ornament and were popular motifs throughout the 'seventies and 'eighties, the sunflower in particular occurring in every conceivable material from cast-iron and brickwork to embroidery 'as if it were the sum total of all beauty'.[3] The lily motif with its fairly obvious symbolism is said to have originated with Rossetti's Blessed Damozel who leant out from the bar of Heaven with three lilies in her hand, but it was also used *ad nauseam* as a subject for design in all media and forms one of the links between aestheticism and Art Nouveau; and of course Rossetti kept peacocks in his London garden.

Another possible origin of the enthusiasm for the lily can also be traced to Oscar Wilde. In 1879 as a young man recently down from Oxford he conceived a great admiration for the society beauty, Lily Langtry. She recorded in her memoirs that Wilde was in the practice of bringing her flowers and on several occasions he visited Covent Garden Market, purchased a single, giant Amaryllis and proceeded down Piccadilly to present the flower to the object of his affections. Lily Langtry reported that this was at the time construed as a pose and the theory is given credence by the famous lines by W. S. Gilbert, written only two years later, about the young man who walked down Piccadilly with a poppy or a lily in his medieval hand.

Oscar Wilde was born in Dublin in 1854 and after a fairly conventional education he went up to Oxford in 1874. There, unlike his fellow undergraduates, he became infected by the current artistic enthusiasms for Pre-Raphaelite painting, for engravings and blue and white porcelain. Before he had been long at Oxford his rooms in Magdalen were popularly considered to be one of the show places of the college and of the university. The three rooms were panelled, he had the ceilings and dados decorated with painted ornament and the walls were hung with old engravings. His considerable collection of blue and white porcelain was housed on shelves and it was at one of his many entertainments in these rooms that Wilde is said to have made the well known remark, 'Oh, would that I could live up to my blue china'. He seems to have worked briefly under Walter Pater, whose influential *Studies in the History of the Renaissance* was published in 1873, and attended Ruskin's lectures on Florentine art. It was these lectures and Ruskin's personal influence that launched Wilde into a veritable crusade for art. Incidentally Wilde, like Ruskin many years earlier, won the Newdigate Prize for English verse, in his case with a weighty work called *Ravenna* celebrating both the splendours of Italian art and the new political unity of Italy.

Wilde himself gave several accounts of how a group of undergraduates attended one of Ruskin's lectures in which the Master expounded on his regrets that the best physique and strength of the young men of England were wasted on the cricket field or the river instead of being directed into noble work that would do good for other people. The audience was so moved that as a result, under Ruskin's direction, they spent some part of the

Fig. 4 Portrait of Oscar Wilde from an original photograph by Elliott & Fry, about 1881. *London, Victoria and Albert Museum.*

following winter building a road between the villages of Upper and Lower Hinksey, divided in those days by a swamp. After two months of hard work Ruskin departed for Venice and the road ended abruptly in the middle of the swamp. Oscar Wilde, however, felt that all the energy previously devoted to the road should be harnessed, as he said, 'to create an artistic movement that might change . . . the face of England. There was none of us idle; poets most of us, so ambitious were we: painters some of us, or workers in metal or modellers, determined that we would try and create for ourselves beautiful work, for those who love us, poems and pictures, and for those who love us not, epigrams and paradoxes and scorn.'[4] With the exception of the sting in the tail for enemies of art, these aims were clearly inspired by the works of Ruskin and William Morris. It was at about this time during 1877 that Morris delivered his first lecture on 'The Decorative Arts' and a number of his ideas appear in Wilde's lectures masquerading as original thought, notably the famous injunction to 'have nothing in your houses which you do not know to be useful or believe to be beautiful'.[5] Despite Wilde's claims there is no evidence that any of his energetic Oxford companions made any more effective contribution to art than they had done to road making but Wilde himself embarked enthusiastically on a career as an art critic and poet.

Coming down from Oxford in 1878 with a brilliant reputation, Wilde's tall, elegant figure and flowing hair made him the personification of a type of the Pre-Raphaelite movement. He was 'the rage' socially and his youth seemed to excuse his pose as an artistic reformer. Wilde in his turn came into contact with some of the figures whom he had admired from afar. He met Burne-Jones through Comyns Carr, the director of the Grosvenor Gallery, and the two became good friends, and for some years he was the constant companion of Whistler who had long been his hero, personifying as he did all the undergraduate theories of living beautifully amongst blue and white porcelain. Their mutual image was so confused in the public mind that Bunthorne, the Fleshly Poet in *Patience*, though intended as a caricature of Wilde, was made up with the black curls, moustache and eye glass of Whistler. During their association Wilde wrote poetic versions of the Thames Nocturne paintings and absorbed many of Whistler's ideas. When he married in 1884 he bought a house in Tite Street, Chelsea, close to Whistler and had it altered, decorated and furnished by their mutual friend, E. W. Godwin. Few of Whistler's friendships lasted long and Wilde and he finally parted company over some suggestion of plagiarism in Wilde's much publicized lectures.

But in the meantime Wilde had made his greatest contribution to the Art Movement – a lecture tour of the United States of America. Interest in the aesthetic school had spread to the United States largely through the influence of such books as Eastlake's *Hints on Household Taste* and cheap reprints of the aesthetic poets. The movement was obviously fairly widely known as *Patience* opened to an appreciative audience in New York only five months after its London première. One contemporary account of the trip suggested that Wilde himself felt that it was necessary to explain real aestheticism to the Americans, as opposed to the stage interpretation, and 'possibly instruct and elevate our rich, clever but not particularly cultured transatlantic cousins'.[6] This attitude was also suggested by the press account of Wilde's departure from England on Christmas Eve 1881 when he declared himself to be carrying culture to a continent armed only with his genius. This rather supercilious view was obviously modified by contact with the transatlantic cousins who were most enthusiastic in their reception of the young lecturer and who proved, en masse, to be better educated than their English counterparts.

An alternative suggestion for the origin of the lecture tour was that it was arranged by D'Oyly Carte to advertise the opera. It seems unlikely that Wilde, even if he was prepared to laugh at himself, would have agreed to be used as an advertising agent for a work which professed to ridicule all that he most admired in both art and poetry. In addition he would appear to have financed the trip himself as he said on arrival in New York that his subsequent movements would depend on the financial success of the first lecture. In fact the lecture tour lasted for eighteen months while *Patience* ran to packed houses in New York and another company took the show on the road. Whatever the original intentions the whole affair was a considerable personal triumph for Oscar Wilde both as prophet of the revived domestic arts and as showman. Thousands flocked to his lectures, crowds gathered at wayside railway stations for a view of this strange European phenomenon and hundreds of copies of his photograph were sold to admirers, and last but not least he inspired popular songs and music. Some of these songs originated in England, such as *Quite Too Utterly Utter, A New Aesthetic Roundelay* and were later also published in the States but most of them were written there for his new admirers. These included *The Oscar Wilde Gallop, Oscar Polka Mazurka* and *Oscar Dear* published by F. W. Helmick of Cincinatti in 1882. The words of this latter song are typical of many of the outpourings in verse form inspired by Wilde's appearance and charm.

> 'I'll sing to you of a nice young man
> Of virtues rich and rare,
> Of stature tall and ankles thin
> And long and curly hair.
> Aesthetic to a great degree
> In actions sweet and mild
> Sublimely lank and nonchalant,
> But just a little wild!

The pictorial covers of this sheet music invariably showed languid young men with lilies, in supposedly artistic settings, or Oscar Wilde himself in his famous knickerbocker suit. There must rarely if ever have been a serious artistic endeavour which so captured the imagination of the great mass of the public at all levels, from the undergraduates of Harvard to the purchasers of popular songs. Wilde's importance in the history of the Aesthetic Movement is in fact a direct result of this popularity which ensured that all his doings were recorded; complete lectures were published in the popular

E·W·Godwin·f·s·a· Architect ·   ×   R·W·Edis·f·s·a· Arch! ·   ×   E·W·Godwin·f·s·a· Architect ·

62

62   Artists' Houses in Chelsea; a view of Tite Street drawn by Thomas Raffles Davison from *The British Architect*, May, 1880.

Overleaf

63   Front elevation of the House and Studio in Tite Street, designed by E. W. Godwin for Mr F. Miles, 1879, as published in *The British Architect*, July 1880.

64   The White House, Tite Street, Chelsea, designed by E. W. Godwin for J. McNeil Whistler, 1878. Revised front elevation, as published in *The British Architect*.

E·W·Godwin·Archt·

C·P·Edwards·del·

SCALE OF 0   5   10   15   20   25 FEET

House & Studio for J·A·M^cN·Whistler Esq·Chelsea

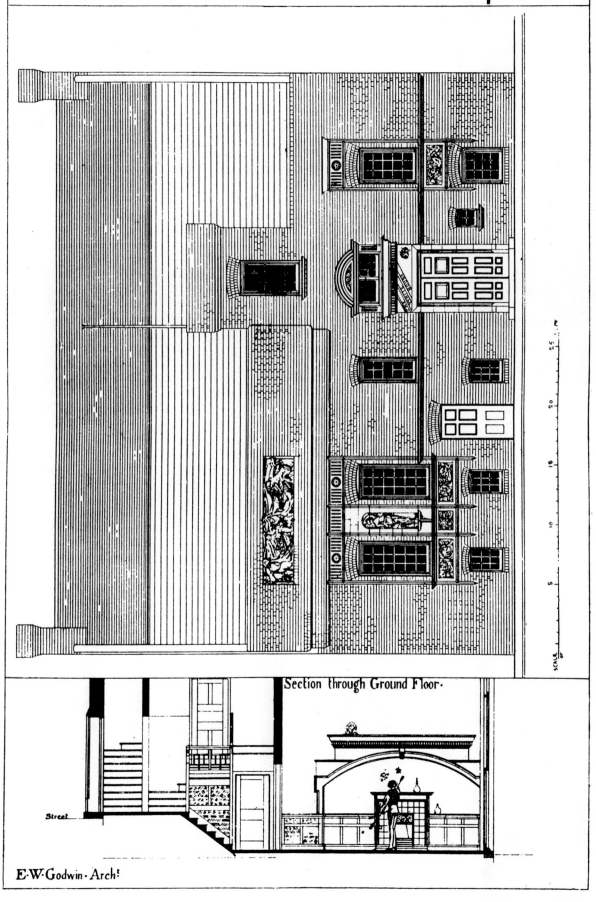

Section through Ground Floor.

Street

E·W·Godwin·Arch^t

65   Wornington Road School
from *School Architecture* by
E. R. Robson, 1874.

66   Cast-iron Pavilion designed
by Thomas Jeckyll and made by
Barnard, Bishop & Barnard,
Norwich, 1876. *British Architect*,
Nov. 1878.

66

ÆSTHETIC LOVE IN A COTTAGE.

Miss Bilderbogie. "YES, DEAREST JOCONDA! I AM GOING TO MARRY YOUNG PETER PILCOX! WE SHALL BE VERY, *VERY* POOR! INDEED HOW WE ARE GOING TO *LIVE*, I CANNOT TELL!"

Mrs. Cimabue Brown. "OH, MY BEAUTIFUL MARIANA, HOW *NOBLE* OF YOU BOTH! NEVER MIND *HOW*, BUT *WHERE* ARE YOU GOING TO LIVE?"

Miss Bilderbogie. "OH, IN DEAR OLD KENSINGTON, I SUPPOSE—EVERYTHING IS SO CHEAP THERE, YOU KNOW!—PEACOCK FEATHERS ONLY A *PENNY A-PIECE!*"

67

67   'Aesthetic Love in a Cottage',
cartoon by George du Maurier
published in *Punch*, Volume 80,
1881.

68   'Sweet Little Buttercup' or
Art Embroidery, cartoon by
Linley Sambourne published in
Punch, Volume 76, 1879.

"SWEET LITTLE BUTTERCUP;"

Or, Art-Embroidery, 1879.

69   Ornament from Liberty's
Eastern Art Catalogue, Dec. 1880.

press while the words of his less flamboyant contemporaries have been lost.

The first lecture on 'The English Renaissance of Art' was given in New York on 9 January 1882, soon after his arrival. The arrival itself was recorded very fully in the New York press and in a splendid burlesque interview in *Punch*. In this the poet was described as 'dressed in a long, snuff-coloured single breasted coat which reached his heels, and was relieved with a seal-skin collar and cuffs rather the worse for wear while a small daisy drooped despondently in his buttonhole'. He was said to be leaning against a chimney piece which had been painted pea green with panels of peacock blue pottery let in at uneven intervals and 'we may state, that the chimney piece as well as the seal-skin collar is the property of Oscar and will appear in his lectures on the Growth of Artistic Taste in England'.[7]

The *New York Tribune*, however, was kind about the lecturer's appearance and enthusiastic enough about the content to print a very long précis on the morning after the lecture and its lead was followed subsequently by other papers. There are numerous versions of these lectures, all of which differ to some extent. This is understandable as in the eighteen-months' tour Wilde lectured in New York, Boston, Omaha, Philadelphia and many other smaller towns before moving to Canada where he spoke in Montreal, Ottawa, Kingston, Quebec and to 1,100 persons in Toronto's Grand Opera House. He seems to have given three basic lectures at all these places: on the 'English Renaissance', 'House Decoration' and 'Art and the Handicraftsman' but they were given from notes and each lecture obviously varied according to the circumstances and the type and size of audience. When the lectures were first published in book form, some years after Wilde's death, the editor found four copies of the first lecture all varying in some degree from each other and from the published press accounts.

However the main burden of the message of the lectures is clear and it can be assumed that it represented the approach of the aesthetes of the 1880s. Wilde was a little muddled in his exposition but the essence of his views was contained in the first lecture – 'Love art for its own sake and then all things that you need will be added to you'. The same lecture concluded with the observation that 'the secret of life is art'. This broad conclusion led logically to every aspect of life being related to art. 'Stately and simple architecture for your cities, bright and simple dress for your men and women; those are the conditions of a real artistic movement. For the artist is not concerned primarily with any theory of life but with life itself.' In Wilde's view a noble work of art could only be produced in a healthy, clean atmosphere and not in the polluted air of grimy industrial cities. From this followed a need for improved social conditions producing healthy young men and women, for 'sickly or idle or melancholy people do not do much in art' or in any other field of creative work. These healthy people in their turn must be individualists and in the last extreme Wilde equated republicanism and socialism with good art, proving his point by derisory reference to the products of France under Louis XIV. He poured scorn on the French decorative arts which had for so long been admired in England. 'The gaudy, gilt furniture writhing under a sense of its own horror and ugliness, with a nymph smirking at every angle and a dragon mouthing on every claw' he attributed directly to the follies of the nobility and monarchy of France. This was obviously a good approach in his attempt to spread culture in republican America and many of his other views were tailored for an American audience.

Wilde was clearly enormously impressed by the natural beauty and size of this new continent. He travelled extensively in the course of his tour and recommended to his audiences the magnificent materials that were available on their own doorsteps. Whereas in England native materials were relatively simple and more exotic things had to be sought abroad, his American audiences had to hand 'marble richer than Pentelicus and more varied than Paros' with which it was wrong merely to build great square houses. The material should be worked by noble workmen into marvellous forms. Similarly the various precious stones could give impetus to much-needed new designs and jewellery and, above all, Wilde suggested that it should be easy for American craftsmen to produce magnificent goldsmiths' work. A little optimistically he declared 'the gold is ready for you in unexhausted treasure, stored up in the mountain hollow or strewn on the river sand, and was not given to you for barren speculation. There should be some better record of it left in your history than the merchant's panic and the ruined home.' Similarly he advocated the use of native flowers and animals as design motifs rather than the repetition of those chosen by Greeks, Goths or even the contemporary Japanese.

These ideas were reiterated in various forms in his American lectures, notably one first given in May 1882 with the cumbersome title 'The Practical Application of the Principles of the Aesthetic Theory to Exterior and Interior House Decoration with Observations upon Dress and Personal Ornaments'. He further encouraged his American audiences by pointing out that the commercial spirit upon which their great cities were based was no barrier to art, as might be supposed, drawing a parallel with the similar spirit which was responsible for the development of the great cities of Renaissance Italy. On the other hand he did not hesitate to chide when he felt the occasion warranted it, for instance telling the citizens of Omaha that their houses were ill-designed and shabbily decorated in poor taste. One of the only recorded instances of difficulty with an audience was in Boston when some sixty Harvard students attended a lecture dressed in imitation of Wilde and 'having lilies in their buttonholes and sunflowers in their hands'. Wilde is recorded as having achieved a real triumph by ignoring the intended affront and offering the students a gift of sculpture for their gymnasium.

While he was clear and precise in his advice to his audiences Wilde's exposition of the origins of the new English Art Movement was somewhat confused. He saw it as an outcome of the combined forces of the French Revolution, the poetry of Keats, some Ruskin, and the Pre-Raphaelite movement, coupled with the more practical work of William Morris, the sum total being 'the union of Hellenism – with the intensified individualism, the passionate colour of the romantic spirit'. Despite his overwhelming enthusiasm he seems never to have fully understood his subject, so that on one occasion he could recommend Queen Anne architecture as being the most suitable for England while saying on another that the secret of all good architecture and furniture was the combination of the Greek line with Oriental phantasy. Side by side with this comparative nonsense comes the advanced idea, and a heretical one for a follower of Morris, that 'all machinery may be beautiful when it is undecorated even. Do not seek to decorate it. We cannot but think all good machinery is graceful, also, the line of strength and the line of beauty being one.'

This sort of original observation gives the lie to some of the accusations of plagiarism by Whistler and others. It is to Wilde that the idea of 'Art for Art's Sake' can be traced, a conception which was completely revolutionary in the 1880s when the content of painting had for so long been more import-ant than the painting itself. In one of his lectures he said 'nor in its primary aspect has painting any more spiritual message for us than a blue tile from the wall of Damascus or a Hitzen vase. It is a beautifully-coloured surface, nothing more, and affects us by no suggestion stolen from philosophy, no pathos pilfered from literature, no feeling filched from a poet, but by its own incommunicable artistic essence.'

After the American trip Wilde continued his lectures in London, dressed rather more conventionally in a good dark suit and well-polished boots but still with the symbolic lily in his lapel. He practised what he had been preaching with great enthusiasm in the decoration of his own home in which the dining-chairs were described by the owner as sonnets in ivory and the table as a masterpiece in pearl; but with his appointment as editor of *The Woman's World* he gradually withdrew from active participation in the movement for which he had worked with such feeling.

Chapter 6

SATIRE AND COMMENT

The rise of the Aesthetic Movement and its impact on everyday life was best recorded in that chronicle of English social history, the periodical *Punch*. In its early days *Punch* virtually disregarded the arts except in so far as some of its elaborate and verbose jokes were set, for instance, at a Royal Academy private view but they might equally have been at a race-meeting or a dinner party. Artistic trappings appeared in the domestic interiors of some cartoons in the mid eighteen-seventies but it was not until 1877, when the movement was well established, that Art made its appearance as a subject of mirth. The preface of the complete volume of that year includes 'China-Mania' and 'Oxford Aesthetics' in the list of assorted movements afflicting England in the fortieth year of Queen Victoria's reign and, in the same volume, there are a number of cartoons by George du Maurier (1834–96) on aesthetic topics, one of which is a fully-developed comment on the idea of art for art's sake. An artistic young man is explaining to what is described as a 'matter-of-fact party' that, despite a repulsive subject, poor drawing and beastly colour, the painting which they are both studying is beautiful.[1] The joke clearly presupposes that *Punch* readers were familiar with this sort of situation and it must have been equally well-known in the United States as most of du Maurier's drawings were pirated or appropriated soon after their appearance in England by American illustrated papers, notably the *New York Daily Graphic*.

In 1877 du Maurier's young man was dressed in conventional town clothing and only the text explained his artistic leanings. It was not until 1879 that du Maurier introduced his famous artistic family, the Cimabue Browns and their aesthetic young friends, Postlethwaite and Maudle. The Browns, mother, father and children, aspired to live an artistic life in which they were guided by their admiration for the poet, Postlethwaite, and the painter, Maudle, who in their turn admired each other and their respective arts. In appearance the artistic pair were based roughly on Wilde and Whistler with a touch of Swinburne. They drooped and were lionized in drawing-rooms filled with spindly black furniture, Japanese fans and screens covered in bulrushes and sunflowers. In due course du Maurier became so absorbed in his creations that their own supposed work began to appear in *Punch*. One such piece was a design, 'A Love Agony', said to be the work of the fictitious Maudle and accompanied by some curious verses by Postlethwaite who was reported to have posed for the picture.[2] Maudle's comments on current affairs appeared in articles in *Punch* in 1880 and 1881 and many readers must have believed that he actually existed. One of du Maurier's most attractive drawings (fig. 5) shows four little girls dressed in Kate Greenaway-style costume with peacock-feathers in their hats proudly carrying sunflowers on their afternoon walk. These are the young Cimabue Browns and more conventionally dressed children attribute their dress and bearing to aesthetic exclusiveness. Many of the jokes about adults were based on the self-assumed superiority of the aesthete busily setting standards by which other less enlightened mortals were to live. On their second appearance in *Punch* the smug little Cimabue Brown children shocked their conventional grandfather by expressing a preference for the National Gallery and Bach's 'glorious Passionsmusik' rather than a proffered trip to the Zoo and a pantomime.[3] du Maurier excused the Philistine grandfather by explaining that he had only recently returned from Ceylon and must presumably have been unaware of the rise of the cult for existing beautifully even amongst young children. Most contemporary evidence suggests that the Aesthetic Movement had reached its peak by the early 1880s and this theory is also supported by du Maurier's drawings (plate 67). Always the most careful observer of the social scene, direct reference to aesthetes had disappeared from his cartoons by 1882 and Postlethwaite and Company withdrew from *Punch* late in 1881 in a short poem entitled *The Downfall of the Dado*.[4] It is in the form of a drawing-room operetta and the stage instructions at the end of each verse describe the breaking of blue and white china, the rending of aesthetic flowers and the final ascent of the company including Maudle, Postlethwaite and Mrs Cimabue Brown from 'The Dismal Depths of Dadocracy to the Coral Caves of Common Sense'. The aesthetes faded quietly from the pages of *Punch*

Fig. 5 'The Height of Aesthetic Exclusiveness', an original drawing by George du Maurier for a cartoon published in *Punch*, Volume 77, 1879. *The caption reads* MAMMA: 'Who are those extraordinary-looking children?' EFFIE: 'The Cimabue Browns, Mamma – they're *Aesthetic*, you know!' MAMMA: 'So I should imagine. Do you know them to speak to?' EFFIE: 'Oh *Dear* no, Mamma – they're most *exclusive* – why, they put out their tongues at us if we only *look* at them!' *London, Victoria and Albert Museum*

Fig. 6 Caricature of Oscar Wilde
by Linley Sambourne from *Punch*,
Volume 80, 1881. *The caption reads*
'O.W.'
'O, I feel just as happy as a bright
sunflower!'
Aesthete of Aesthetes!
What's in a name?
The poet is WILDE,
But his poetry's tame.
London, Victoria and Albert Museum

though the arts, and in particular the amateur artist, remained as subjects for cartoons and jokes.

The other *Punch* artist most concerned with witticisms at the expense of aesthetes was Edward Linley Sambourne (1844–1910). Unlike du Maurier, who relied for his work on the careful observation of society and coupled his drawings with verbose jokes, Linley Sambourne (1844–1910) worked almost entirely from imagination producing what were described as quaint and fanciful drawings with captions so brief that the editors of *Punch* sometimes provided explanations for their less quick-witted readers. Thus a portrait of O. W. (fig. 6) as a sunflower was accompanied by an editorial note explaining that this particular 'Fancy Portrait' was of Oscar Wilde. Linley Sambourne's first sunflower appeared without comment in the Almanac for 1877 and his subsequent political cartoons and fanciful drawings often had an aesthetic note. One of the most successful and self-explanatory drawings poked fun at 'Art Embroidery' (plate 68). This shows a charming young lady dressed rather suggestively in a William Morris type fabric surrounded by the paraphernalia of contemporary embroidery. *Punch* derived a lot of simple fun from the possibilities of combining aesthetic enthusiasms with fashion, such as the lady who carried her feeling for blue and white porcelain to the lengths of wearing applied plates on her gown and a delicate little teapot on her head (fig. 7). Linley Sambourne's own position in relation to the Art Movement was somewhat ambiguous. The evidence suggests that in 1877 it became editorial policy to attack aesthetes in *Punch* much as it had previously dealt ruthlessly with other movements and individuals. Sambourne, who worked for the paper, obviously conformed with its views but his own house which was decorated and furnished in 1874 remains today as one of the most perfect examples of an artistic interior (plates 49, 58). There are Morris wallpapers, art embroideries, art furniture, Japanese ornaments from Liberty's and decorations designed by Linley Sambourne himself. The main feature of the drawing-room is a handsome stained-glass window in which birds flit amongst giant sunflowers and potted palms.

Quite apart from providing visual copy for his one-time friend, du Maurier, Whistler was an early butt for *Punch* in its literary campaign against the aesthetes. The 1877 volume contained a poem on Whistler's newly completed Peacock Room (plate 59) as well as a series of rather puerile suggestions for future paintings such as 'a depravity in scarlet, an impertinence in any colour or an optical illusion in invisible green'. The Peacock Room theme recurred over the years, culminating in a poem published in 1881, the first verse of which ran:

'Her blue-green dress on the grey-blue floor
    Lay in folds all tumbled and hilly,
Like the waves that break on the smooth sea shore
    Or the crumpled leaves of a floating lily.'

From this example it can be deduced that the literary standard maintained by *Punch* was by no means equal to that of its drawings. Verse was one of its most popular weapons for satire but it was of a poor quality, except on the rare occasions when it was actual parody. One of the more successful pieces in this vein was a parody of the poem by Edward Waller *Go Lovely Rose*:

CHINAMANIA MADE USEFUL AT LAST!

Fig. 7 'Chinamania made useful at last!' from *Punch*, Volume 78, 1880. *London, Victoria and Albert Museum*

The Aesthete and the Rose

Go flaunting Rose!
Tell her that wastes her love on thee,
    That she nought knows,
Of the new Cult Intensity,
If sweet and fair to her you be.

    Tell her that's young,
Or who in health and bloom takes pride,
    That bards have sung
Of a new youth – at whose sad side
    Sickness and pallor aye abide.

    Small is the worth
Of Beauty in crude charms attired,
    She must shun mirth,
Have suffered fruitlessly and desired,
And wear no flush by hope inspired.

    Then die, that she
May learn that death is passing fair,
    May read in thee
How little of Art's praise they share
    Who are not sallow sick and spare.[5]

The pale, sad and melancholy manner adopted by would-be aesthetes gave infinite scope to the satirists. To indicate right-thinking it seemed necessary to droop limply in imitation of the pale characters in Pre-Raphaelite paintings. *The Decorative Sisters*, an amusing little book on this subject, was published in New York in 1882 (plate 107). The format was similar to that of children's books of the time but in this case it was directed at aesthetically-minded adults and told the sad story of two previously ordinary young ladies who became 'intense' and spent their days sketching sunflowers and looking at lilies instead of pursuing a healthy, rural life.

Some of the artistic jokes in *Punch* which may well have been amusing at the time have misfired in the long run. In the same volume in which cartoons ridiculed the possibility of flying from London to Paris or bottling and storing music for later enjoyment, *Punch* published an Art Utilitarian Examination Paper. The questions ranged from designs for posters and suggestions for the best way of advertising a new soup to the conversion of a stucco villa into a Queen Anne Mansion. Today no one would think it strange that a student should be required to design a poster or promote the sale of soup and the basic joke, that the applied arts might ever be a subject of higher education, has proved to be very wide of the mark.

F. C. Burnand (1836–1917) became the editor of *Punch* at the height of its campaign of ridicule aimed at art in general and aesthetes in particular. Realizing that the subject was still popular with the public he wrote a play or, to be more precise, converted an existing French one, in which the aesthetic characters were represented not only as fools but as knaves. The joke would seem to have failed to some extent because the sets and costumes, at which the audience were expected to laugh, were so attractive that several critics regarded the play *The Colonel* as an excellent advertisement for aestheticism. After seeing the play E. W. Godwin wrote that the set 'presented to us as wrong, we find is furnished with artistic and simple things; a charming cabinet in walnut designed by Mr Padgett for the green room, some simple inexpensive Sussex chairs like those sold by Messrs W. Morris and Co., a black coffee table after the well known example originally designed in 1867 by the writer of these notes; a quite simple writing table, matting on the floor, a green and yellow paper on the walls, a sunflower frieze, a Japanese treatment of the ceiling and a red sun such as we see in Japanese books, and a hand screen, make up a scene which if found wanting in certain details and forced in sunflowers, is certainly an intriguing room with individuality about it, quiet in tone and what is most important, harmonious and pleasing.' He also reported seeing the leading lady outside the theatre where she passed unnoticed though 'her private costume was modelled line for line on that she had just worn as an aesthete in the comedy, and which the audience had been invited to ridicule'.[6]

This view of *The Colonel* (see plate 97) was taken by other and presumably more detached commentators such as the dramatic critic of *The London Illustrated News* whose enthusiasm was such that he visited the play twice in the first month of its production, February 1881, and wrote about it at length on both occasions. He thought the plot trivial but found the performance excellent and the settings and costumes the best that had been seen on the London stage for many years. This anonymous critic, not unnaturally, took exception to the suggestion implicit in the play that an admiration for the work of the artists of the Italian Renaissance automatically led to the picking of pockets or the telling of lies. He was, however, delighted by the subtle education of the Philistines who came all unsuspecting to enjoy a gay evening in the theatre little thinking that they were absorbing the philosophy at which they were laughing. The critic felt that the whole thing was quite harmless because in his view culture was rapidly winning the day 'over stupid and vulgar Philistinism'. The play had a long and successful run in London and in the autumn of 1881 gained the distinction of a Royal Command performance before Queen Victoria at Abergeldie Castle in Scotland. The new ideas were so generally accepted by this time that it was reported that furniture for the aesthetic scene was purchased expressly in Edinburgh to save the cost of transport from London and additional pieces were borrowed from the Prince and Princess of Wales.

Dramatic entertainments were not the exclusive prerogative of the aesthetic opposition. In 1875 Comyns Carr, friend of many artists and director of the Grosvenor Gallery in London, the shop window of aesthetic painters, helped in the production of *A Cabinet of Secrets* at St George's Hall

70 'Marigolds and Blossom', chintz designed by B. J. Talbert and roller printed in colours by Stead, McAlpin & Co., 1873. *London, Public Record Office.*

72

71 'Sunflowers and Vetch',
chintz designed by B. J. Talbert
and roller printed in colours by
James Back, Glasgow, 1875.
London, Public Record Office.

72 'Flower Pot' panel,
embroidered in coloured silks on
white flannel and designed by
William Morris about 1880.
London, Victoria and Albert Museum.

in Portland Place. This was a small hall or theatre which specialized in 'select' and intimate entertainments, in character somewhere between domestic charades and musical plays. *A Cabinet of Secrets* was a skit on china collecting, a pastime of the *élite*, which by the mid-seventies had assumed the proportions of a fashionable craze. The theme song of the piece concluded with the line 'we revel in the form and glaze of every cup and saucer' and the plot was based on the idea that a world-wide passion for porcelain might break down international barriers and ultimately cure the ills of the world. It would appear that 'select' artistic audiences were quite prepared to laugh at their own enthusiasms.

The culmination of all the aesthetic fun was the production of Gilbert and Sullivan's new comic opera *Patience or Bunthorne's Bride* at the Opera Comique in London on St George's Day, 1881. Subtitled 'An Aesthetic Opera', it was an immediate success, acknowledged by all but the *Punch* critic who ignored its very existence, presumably because he regarded the opera as unfair competition for *The Colonel*. Richard D'Oyly Carte, the impresario, had already had some years of success with Gilbert and Sullivan's comic operas but *Patience* was to be a milestone in his career. With its 'Fleshly and Idyllic Poets', chorus of lovesick maidens in aesthetic draperies playing mandolins and, of all improbable things, 'cellos, it exactly fitted the mood of the times. The text was witty enough to amuse the converted and cruel enough for the Philistines. As in *The Colonel* before it, while the aesthetes were held up to ridicule, the costumes were elegantly and genuinely artistic. These were designed by the author himself, W. S. Gilbert (1836–1911), and made from fashionable Liberty textiles which were actually advertised on theatre programmes printed in the fashionable asymmetrical Japanese way. After a successful run at the Opera Comique in London, D'Oyly Carte elected to open his new Savoy Theatre, itself an artistic landmark, with the same opera but, as he announced, with 'new scenery, costumes and increased chorus'.

Opened on 14 October 1881, the Savoy Theatre had the distinction of being the first public building 'lit permanently and in all departments' with electric light. A gas supply was available in case of emergencies though it does not seem to have been necessary to use it. The theatre was artistically decorated in keeping with the times with rich embossed wallpaper in tones of Venetian red and the seating upholstered in peacock blue plush in the stalls and stamped velvet for the rest of the house. The only other colour used was a pale, soft yellow and the usual painted drop scene was replaced by a gold satin curtain.

The real innovation was the almost simultaneous opening in London and New York of the same comic opera. Earlier Gilbert and Sullivan pieces such as *H.M.S. Pinafore* had been ruthlessly pirated in the United States and D'Oyly Carte decided to overcome this complimentary but financially unrewarding practice by launching an official version before sub-standard productions could get under way. To this end the Carte Bureau was established in New York conveniently near to the Standard Theatre and a publicity campaign was launched. So successful was the new venture that during the latter part of 1881 and the whole of 1882 D'Oyly Carte had two

73 'Peacock', wallpaper designed by E. W. Godwin and hand-printed by Jeffrey & Co., 1873. *London, Public Record Office.*

74 Wallpaper, anonymously designed, printed by Corbiere, Son & Brindle, 1877. *London, Public Record Office.*

75 'Nagasaki', silk damask made by Warner & Sons about 1874, and probably designed by E. W. Godwin. *London, Victoria and Albert Museum.*

76 Upholstery fabric in worsted wool and silk by an unknown designer, about 1880. *London, Victoria and Albert Museum.*

77 Detail of a piano cover embroidered in gold thread and *appliqué* on silk damask, designed by C. R. Ashbee, about 1889. *London, Victoria and Albert Museum.*

Fig. 8 Monogram of Richard D'Oyly Carte combined with the sunflower, Union Jack and Stars and Stripes from the programme published by the Standard Theatre, New York, on the occasion of the 100th performance of *Patience. London, Victoria and Albert Museum*

Patience companies touring England in addition to the London production and in America there was a company at the Standard Theatre, New York, as well as a touring company. So close was the liaison between the two productions that on 29 December 1881 a souvenir programme was published celebrating jointly the 250th London show and the 100th in New York. But, despite all the precautions, two pirate companies were also presenting *Patience* in Chicago. Clearly aesthetes were prevalent enough in the United States to be found amusing.

Always at his best as a satirist, W. S. Gilbert produced some of his most sparkling writing in *Patience* and dealt with almost every aspect of the art craze. It is made quite plain throughout the whole piece that to be fashionably aesthetic it was necessary to droop despairingly, and to be visibly soulfully intense. The contrast between aesthetes and the others was made the more pointed in that their rivals for the affection of the rapturous maidens of the chorus were army officers whose attentions were rebuffed initially because their uniforms were of gay, bright primary colours. It was suggested to the Dragoons that they would be altogether more attractive dressed in 'a cobwebby grey velvet, with a tender bloom like a cold gravy, which, made Florentine fourteenth century, trimmed with Venetian leather and Spanish altar lace, and surmounted with something Japanese – would at least be Early English.' This recipe could have been taken from almost any contemporary book on decoration but for the typically Gilbertian deflationary note introduced by the cold gravy.

At one point Bunthorne, the Fleshly Poet, admits to the audience in a recitative and song that he has no real love for languid lilies or things Japanese and that his whole attitude is a pose 'born of a morbid love of admiration'. He then gives a most useful list of requirements for those wishing to appear cultured, including what could almost be described as the fashionable architect's motto –

'Be eloquent in praise of the very dull old days which have long since passed away,
And convince 'em if you can, that the reign of good Queen Anne was Culture's palmiest day.'

The transformation of the Dragoons into acceptably fashionable young men gave Gilbert the opportunity to pour scorn on the taste for the medieval, for blue and white china, lilies and all the other trimmings of the movement and he concluded with a sparkling lyric pinpointing the whole fashionable craze:

'A Japanese young man,
A blue and white young man,
Francesca di Rimini, miminy, piminy,
Je-ne-sais-quoi young man!

A pallid and thin young man,
A haggard and lank young man
A greenery-yallery, Grosvenor Gallery,
Foot-in-the-grave young man!'

Scornful though they may have been, others cashed in on the whole affair. The eminently respectable Worcester Royal Porcelain Company took the opportunity to issue a remarkable teapot composed of the head and torso of a male and a female back to back dressed in costumes derived from the stage presentation of *Patience* (plate 101) and inscribed underneath 'Fearful consequences through the laws of Natural Selection and Evolution of living up to one's teapot'. It was an expensive and complicated but apparently successful joke. The pot is actually beautifully and ingeniously modelled, the elegantly drooping arms of the figures providing the spout through which the tea was poured. Both parties wear 'yallery' green garments with puce hats and both have fashionable red hair.

Patience ran in London for 578 performances and though it provided excellent entertainment it did considerable disservice to the serious aspects of the Art Movement, as did all the other public jibes at the outward appearances of the fashionable few. *The British Architect*, one of the periodicals which led the way in serious design reform in many fields, chose the occasion of the 500th performance to philosophize on the little that had been achieved thus far. 'If there is nothing else to illustrate the fact, the sickening repetition of the sunflower in all sorts of decorative work (as though it were the sum total of all beauty) would be enough to show how little the general public have yet derived from the increased study of art.'[7]

Chapter 7

'ART' INDUSTRY

Initially one of the motivating forces of the Aesthetic Movement was the antipathy of the art world to the products of industry and the machine but, ironically enough, by the early 1870s 'art' was becoming a profitable adjunct of many an established business. Trade was imitating what had been begun by artist-craftsmen and by 1880 the movement had snowballed to such an extent that any successful retailer or maker of household goods included the word 'art' somewhere in the description of his business. In the early stages in the late 1860s there seem to have been certain hazards in the art business. Trade periodicals record a number of short-lived firms, such as the first of the Art Furniture Companies with which E. W. Godwin was associated and which began and ended in 1867, and Christopher Dresser's 'Art Furniture Alliance'. This was a showroom in New Bond Street for the sale of metalwork, furniture and other objects mostly designed by Dresser himself and 'attendants robed in many aesthetic costumes of the period, in demure art colours, added a certain air to the place, which set it absolutely apart from a shop'.[1] It must have been so unlike any other shop that it was not a successful commercial venture. However by the late '70s, art was no longer a risk. Trade directories list dozens of Art Furniture Manufacturers and Art Metal Workers and other trades, many of which were old-established firms who thought it politic to add 'art' to their other activities. W. B. Simpson, the tile- and glass-makers, became art tile painters in 1873. In 1876 Gillow and Company listed themselves both as cabinet-makers and as Art Furniture Manufacturers and many other firms followed suit. In 1880, Walter Crane, whose business abilities seem always to have equalled his skill as a designer, became Art Superintendent of the London Decorating Company, a firm with a capital of £100,000, specializing in encaustic tiles. The prospectus of the new company showed Art, Science and Health as the three graces. Walter Crane and many others were able successfully to combine commerce and arts and crafts.

In some cases tradesmen merely produced parodies of fashionable designs or conventional goods in supposed art colours. In 1880 one firm produced a series of 'Early English' leather goods 'of a new tint of green called Elizabethan'. An entry in the same year in *The Artist* recorded that Messrs William Collins, makers of wood and fancy boxes, were making a 'Queen Anne' writing desk fitted with 'the new sea-green Queen Anne notepaper and sundries'. It is difficult to visualize the subtle difference between these two new and original royal greens. Other firms made and sold goods genuinely inspired by the real spirit of the new movement. Pottery, textiles, wallpapers, silver and furniture of quality, which have had a lasting effect on design, were made between 1870 and 1885.

The first and most important of these enterprises was William Morris's own firm. It was established in April 1861 with the name Morris, Marshall, Faulkner and Company as a direct result of Morris's personal furnishing difficulties. Finding nothing that pleased him on the market, he and his friends set to and designed their own furniture, embroideries and wallpaper. The firm had its first modest success at the 1862 International Exhibition in London at which goods were sold to the value of £131. The business moved to its own premises at 26 Queen Square in 1865, was renamed Morris and Company in 1875, in April 1877 opened showrooms in Oxford Street, London, and in 1881 showrooms were opened in New York,[2] slightly predating the arrival of Oscar Wilde and *Patience*. Morris and Company were both retailers and manufacturers, or at least supervisors of the manufacture of the goods they sold. Cabinet furniture was made in their own small workshops and the well-known chairs were made to the firm's specifications probably at High Wycombe. All the wallpapers were printed by the leading art wallpaper firm, Jeffrey and Company, who also worked for a number of other retailers and designers. Both woven and printed textiles were ultimately made in the Morris workshops at Merton Abbey, which were taken over in 1881, but in the earlier years of the firm the designs were woven or printed on commission by outside firms. Silks were woven at Macclesfield and wool tapestries and lenos made by Alexander Morton at Darvel in Scotland. Before Morris embarked on the weaving of hand-knotted pile carpets himself, his earliest carpet designs were for machine-produced floor coverings made by the Heckmondwike Manufacturing Company in Yorkshire and the Wilton Royal Carpet Works. The earliest chintzes were printed on commission in about 1868–70 and after his experiments with vegetable dyes some printing on silk was done at Leek by Thomas Wardle. But the bulk of Morris's textile dyeing and printing was carried out after the establishment of the firm's own workshops at Merton Abbey. The only part of the company's activities almost exclusively executed on their own premises from the inception was embroidery, though some of the more elaborate designs were worked by skilled needle-women amongst Morris's clients. In addition to actual embroideries the firm supplied patterns traced on cloth or silk and either sold their own specially-dyed silks and wools or advised on the colours to be used.

The retailer whose name has remained most closely associated with the Aesthetic Movement is, of course, Liberty. In addition to the oriental goods that Liberty's originally imported and sold, the business was expanded to include the sale of pottery, textiles and metalwork, designed and made exclusively for their various shops both in England and abroad, and their influence on the art world continued into the Art Nouveau period. The Italian name of the later movement, 'Stile Liberty', derived from the popular identification on the Continent of Liberty's with the flowing curves of Art Nouveau.

Fig. 9 Drawings of some 'Burmantofts Pottery' made for Messrs Howell & James, from the *British Architect*, October 7, 1881.

Possibly the largest business in London concerned with art manufactures was that of Howell and James of Lower Regent Street. By the mid 'seventies their galleries were the gathering place of artists of all kinds and their annual show of 'Painting on Pottery and Porcelain', instituted in 1875, seems to have rivalled the Royal Academy as a social and artistic event of the London Season. Established as early as 1820, Howell and James sold both antique and modern silver and jewellery as well as most of the requirements of the fashionable furnishing trades. By the early 1860s they had their own pottery mark and by the 1870s they described themselves as 'Silk Mercers and Proprietors of an Art Pottery Gallery' and, in another trade list, as Art Metal Workers. While Howell and James had their own metal workshops most of their other Art products were made on their behalf by other manufacturers. Their stand at the Paris Exhibition of 1878 included lace and various wooden articles in addition to the pottery for which they were well known by this time. The pottery was in every case made by some reputable firm, such as Minton or Doulton, but marked with the Howell and James mark, and they also patronized individual art potteries, such as that of Charles H. Brannum of Barnstaple. While the firm was internationally 'known for their efforts to popularize works of high art and good taste' their secondary purpose was a social one 'to supply graceful, appropriate and at the same time profitable employment for ladies'.

The employment of female labour in their pottery painting establishment seems to have grown from the annual exhibitions at which both amateurs and professionals showed and competed for prizes. The standing of the whole enterprise can be gauged from the fact that the first prize for amateurs in 1878 was presented by the Crown Princess of Germany and was won by the Countess of Warwick for a dish painted with a charming head set against apple blossom. The second prize-winner on this occasion was a professional painter whose plate was exhibited at Paris and subsequently acquired by the Kunstgewerbemuseum in Berlin (plate 82). The exhibitions were judged by members of the Royal Academy and it appears that some attempt was made to divide the prizes equally between amateur and professional painters. The most popular vehicles for decoration were large dishes or plaques, some as much as a yard in diameter, and the subject matter was as diverse as in any contemporary exhibition of painting with landscape subjects, often including children, heading the list of popularity. One of the leading professional artists in this field was a Mrs Sparkes, wife of the head of the Lambeth School of Art, a school much concerned with the development of Art Pottery. Her work was usually exhibited *hors concours* and it was said to be as freely painted as if it would have been on canvas. In addition to decorated and painted wares, Howell and James also sold blanks and colours for both over- and under-glaze painting for amateurs. It seems possible that some of these blanks had designs traced on them ready for colouring but Howell and James usually confined themselves to suggesting suitable subjects, such as the copying of Walter Crane's picture-books for the decoration of a nursery.

Another professional artist and designer associated with the firm was Lewis F. Day (1845–1910). He produced a series of formal designs for plates and vases which he painted himself. In addition he designed a range of 'Early English' and 'Queen Anne' clocks in ebonized wood – one of Howell and James's most distinctive 'art' lines. The faces, in blue and white earthenware, were designed by Day (plate 45) and by R. Phené Spiers and Walter Crane. These were intended to accompany the ubiquitous ebonized and painted cabinets of the artistic home.

W. B. Simpson and Sons were established in London as housepainters and decorators in 1833. In the nature of their work they were involved with tiles and other decorative materials and eventually they became agents for the sale of these goods. By 1873 the business seems to have expanded considerably and W. B. Simpson and Sons described themselves, amongst other things, as 'art tile painters' and 'art glass painters'. With a large showroom in St Martin's Lane, they not only painted tiles but commissioned distinguished designers to work for them. Tile blanks were made by Minton Hollins and by Maw and Company of Jackfield in Shropshire and were painted, glazed and fired on Simpson's premises at 456 West Strand. The decorated tiles were marked with W. B. Simpson's own mark. Unfortunately much of the design was anonymous, like the attractive tiles in the Kunstgewerbemuseum in Berlin (plate 33) which were included in Simpson's display at the Paris Exhibition of 1878. This particular set of tiles is very freshly painted and illustrates craftsmen in an idealized medieval setting busy at their various pursuits. Narrative tiles of this type were particularly popular in the 1880s in fireplace surrounds, some being designed for the purpose and others using subjects from children's books illustrated by such artists as Kate Greenaway (plate 105) and Walter Crane (see also plate 46). In addition to tile painting W. B. Simpson were responsible for the actual tile and mosaic work in a number of important buildings, in particular the tiled refreshment room and grill room at the Victoria and Albert Museum decorated in 1874. This latter room included a series of large figure subjects designed by E. J. Poynter (1836–1919), as well as a series of more routine tiles on which the inevitable sunflower was painted in blue and white. Messrs Jeffrey and Company of Islington printed a set of wallpapers exclusively for W. B. Simpson, notably those designed by Lewis F. Day of which one of the most attractive was the 'Apple Blossom' (plate 10). The wallpapers, like the tiles, were marked with the Simpson monogram. A commentator on the Paris Exhibition of 1878 described the W. B. Simpson exhibits as being 'of much grace, originality and beauty as well as being examples of pure and good Art'.

While some manufacturers and retailers were temporarily involved with the needs of their aesthetic customers, the Art Movement made an enduring impression on English pottery. During the last thirty years of the nineteenth century there was a clear division between ordinary commercial production on the one hand and 'art' pottery, the forerunner of modern studio pottery on the other. In most industries the term 'art' implied a new approach to decoration or design but in some branches of the pottery industry it implied a radical change in methods of production based on the principles of the Arts and Crafts Movement, with its dual respect for the nature of materials and the dignity of the individual craftsman. The established firms, such as

Minton's, Copeland's and the Worcester Royal Porcelain Company, produced highly-finished, sophisticated wares often of considerable elaboration based on increasing technical efficiency. In addition, though the English designers had come to the fore in the 1860s, this was the one industry which continued to rely heavily on foreigners particularly for prestige exhibition work. Current fashions were reflected in some painted decoration but had virtually no effect on shapes, with the exception of some of the Japanese-inspired porcelain made at Worcester, and the occasional oddity such as the Worcester 'Patience' teapot (plates 101,103).

The first actual art pottery was saltglaze stoneware made by Doulton of Lambeth and exhibited at the International Exhibition held in London in 1871. Doulton had been making ornamental flasks, and a variety of basic domestic equipment in brown stoneware, from the early part of the century. The brown material with its rough surface had become increasingly un-popular with the mid-Victorian public who preferred the comparative sophistication of porcelain or white earthenware so that by the middle of the century production was confined to oven-ware and large containers of various kinds. An important new development occurred in the 1860s after John Sparkes, headmaster of a flourishing School of Art at Lambeth, became a friend of Henry Doulton, the head of the firm. Sparkes was later appointed as the Principal of the National Art Training School at South Kensington and his wife was one of the best known of the professional art pottery painters. As a result of this personal association, Doulton embarked on the novel experiment of allowing selected students from the School of Art to work on stoneware, under the direction of John Sparkes.

The pottery was thrown and turned by skilled craftsmen and from their production vessels were selected for decoration by the students, each of whom signed his or her finished work. This practice continued at Doulton for some years and one of the results is that their pots are of particular interest to collectors. Each designer's work can be recognized and identified by the individual marks, usually composed of initials. A group of decorated saltglaze stoneware was first shown to the public at the International Exhibition of 1871 and George Wallis, the Keeper of the Art Collections at South Kensington, wrote of them with considerable enthusiasm. 'The forms are admirable, and the decorations, whether incised or in relief, are always thoroughly well considered, and especially adapted to the material, the mode of production and the use of the object. There are no affected imitations of antique types. The spirit of true design is caught with admirable perception and insight; and it is not too much to say that in Messrs Doulton's case of stoneware in the Pottery Gallery there is not an article that can be deemed in any sense common-place. When colour is introduced it is done sparingly, and with a view to enhance the form of the object and the natural beauty of the material, rather than to conceal the one or the other.' This is high praise for any new venture but the Doulton's saltglaze stoneware of the period incorporated all the aesthetic virtues. Another writer on the same occasion even went so far as to say that 'in many cases they merit the high favour of those who collect pure works of Art'. The production of saltglaze stoneware was peculiarly suited to the combined

78   79

78   Teapot; porcelain, transfer
printed in blue and made by the
Worcester Royal Porcelain Works,
1877. *In the author's possession.*

79   'Bamboo and Fan',
earthenware plate, transfer
printed and painted in enamel
colours. The design was registered
Dec. 1875 and made by Minton's,
with the factory date mark of
April 1880. *In the author's
possession.*

82

80   Pressed glass bowl in the cream colour known as 'Patent Queen's Ware', made by Sowerby & Company, Gateshead, 1879. *London, Victoria and Albert Museum.*

81   Pressed glass dish in 'Patent Queen's Ware', made by Sowerby & Company, Gateshead, and probably designed by J. G. Sowerby, dated Feb. 1879. *London, Victoria and Albert Museum.*

82   Plate made by Minton's for Howell & James, painted by Edith S. Hall and signed and dated 1877. *West Berlin, Kunstgewerbemuseum.*

83   Plate from the 'Sparrow and Bamboo' service, earthenware with moulded and transfer printed decoration. The design was registered April 1879 and made by Wedgwood. *In the author's possession.*

83

84 Vase of earthenware painted
by Katherine B. Smallfield and
made by Doulton's, 1884.
London, Victoria and Albert Museum.

85 Jug in saltglaze stoneware.
The design was registered in 1877
and made by Pinder, Bourne & Co.
London, Victoria and Albert Museum.

86 'Yeddo', saltglaze stoneware
jug. The design was registered in
Jan. 1879 and made by
W. Brownfield. *In the author's
possession.*

85

87

88

87   Jug in saltglaze stoneware,
designed by Frank A. Butler, 1882,
and made by Doulton's in
Lambeth. *London, Doulton & Co.
Ltd.*

88   Jug in saltglaze stoneware,
designed by George Tinworth
about 1870, and made by Doulton's
in Lambeth. *London, Doulton & Co.
Ltd.*

89

90

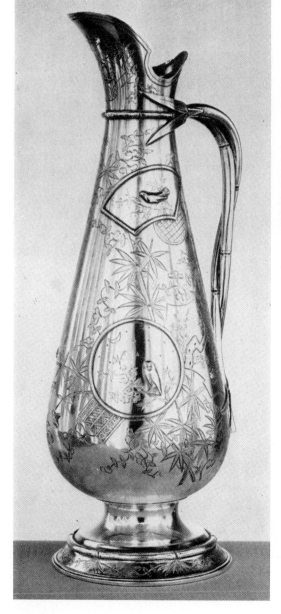

89 Wine jug in silver with
engraved and applied ornament;
Birmingham hallmark for 1880 and
maker's mark of Frederick
Elkington. *London, Victoria and
Albert Museum.*

90 Jug in silver with engraved
decoration; London hallmark for
1881–2 and maker's mark of
John Aldwinkle and James Slater.
London, Victoria and Albert Museum.

91　Jug in saltglaze stoneware with incised and coloured decoration by Emily J. Edwards, and made by Doulton's, 1871. *London, Victoria and Albert Museum.*

92　Plates in earthenware, transfer printed and painted. The design was registered in March 1870. Printed mark on the reverse is 'W. S. Coleman. Inv. & del.' and 'Minton' impressed. *Mrs Barbara Morris.*

92

efforts of technically unskilled students and skilled artisans, as the firing was completed in a single operation and all the decoration was carried out while the pot was in the clay state. This gave considerable freedom of expression to the individual artist. Most of the pottery was moulded in relief, some artists chose to use applied slip decoration, others stamped or impressed ornament and others used freely-drawn incised line emphasized with colour (plate 87). For technical reasons colour was limited to shades of blue and brown but these had a satisfactory quality in their relationship with the clay and were in keeping with the aesthetic demand for soft, earth colours, in marked contrast to the sharp colours of commercial porcelain decoration. One of the earliest and best known of Doulton artists was Hannah B. Barlow who specialized in incised or sgraffito animal subjects, drawn freely on straight-sided vessels. By modern standards Hannah Barlow's representational work bears little relationship to the pottery but it was much admired for its freedom of expression. Some of the most attractive pottery produced by the Lambeth studio were the small pieces by another female artist, Emily J. Edwards (plate 91). She specialized in leaf motifs, directly related to the form of the pottery and set off by boldly-drawn formal background ornament, a type of design found in the best of contemporary wallpaper and textile design and almost certainly derived from the study of Japanese ornament. A key pattern which could almost be described as the trade mark of art pottery, and which was used by a number of Doulton artists, was composed of applied beads or dots of white slip emphasizing the main lines of a design (plate 88). Following the success of the saltglaze stoneware, Doulton enlarged the scope of their Art Studio and introduced Lambeth Faience. This was earthenware painted in colours with a brush at the biscuit stage and the success of this new type of art pottery was said to have inspired Howell and James to organize their exhibitions of painting on pottery. Doulton Art Pottery of both kinds was shown with great success at all the international exhibitions of the 1870s, notably the Philadelphia Centennial, at which they were awarded a number of medals for their work, and at Paris in 1878, when it was written that 'the exquisitely chaste and delicate tints and the wealth of artistic feeling, which pervade these new productions . . . have won for them a fame which will assuredly endure so long as beauty is valued or art is cherished.'[3]

In 1871 at approximately the same time as Doulton's new venture, Minton and Company opened their Art Pottery Studios in South Kensington. Ground was leased from Her Majesty's Commissioners for the Exhibition of 1851 and Minton's built a studio and a kiln 'so arranged as to consume its own smoke'[4] with the intention of persuading eminent artists, 'especially ladies', to paint on porcelain and majolica. It is curious that all the art pottery enterprises seem to lay emphasis on the employment of female artists and painters. The nucleus of the workers at the Minton Art Studio was a group of male professional artists from their factory at Stoke-on-Trent where the biscuit pottery was made and from where it was then transferred to London for decoration and final firing. In addition to its technical equipment the Studio was provided with every amenity to attract and encourage decorative artists in their work. The inspiration of both

Fig. 10 Drawings of 'Burmantofts Pottery' available at Messrs Howell & James's in Regent Street, from *The British Architect*, October 7, 1881.

nature and art were to hand: the Studio adjoined the gardens of the Royal Horticultural Society and was near to both the South Kensington Museum collections and to the School of Art. The Studio manager, William Stephen Coleman (1829–1904), was an artist who began his professional life as a naturalist but had already moved to pottery painting and had had at least one exhibition of his work in this medium before the opening of the Minton Studios. His work had been acclaimed as 'High Art' and a worthy example for others to emulate. While Coleman's boldly painted figure subjects were much admired, they contributed relatively little to the development of art pottery, as can be judged from the fact that his designs were used quite arbitrarily on plates (plate 92), greeting cards or any other art product (plate 106). The wares produced here were normally impressed with the mark 'Minton's Art-Pottery Studio, Kensington Gore', to distinguish them from the normal production at Stoke. Unfortunately it has not proved possible to discover the identity of many of the Minton Studio artists, such as the painter of obvious skill, identified only by the initials E.J.S., who painted a handsome portrait of a fashionable young lady, and enriched it with applied slip, on a large dish or charger (plate 104). The Studio soon became one of the show places of London but unfortunately the venture was only short lived. Coleman left in 1873 and the premises were destroyed by fire in 1875. Though the Studio was not rebuilt, as there was a fairly close association between Doulton and Minton, some of the artists continued their painting on Doulton's Faience.

Wilcock and Company of Leeds were makers of drain-pipes and fire-bricks but in the late 1870s, no doubt inspired by Doulton's example and that of other firms who had 'striven to bring Art to bear on their commoner produce', they embarked on a new art ware, Burmantofts Faience.

The body was of fine clay, found locally, and all the wares relied for their decoration on elaborate modelling and rich, brilliantly coloured glazes. They were stocked by Howell and James and despite their elaborate form were much admired in aesthetic circles. The artist and commentator, T. Raffles Davison, wrote in *The British Architect* in 1881 that 'those aesthetes who can get pitched up high with exquisite sensitive emotion of colour, will do well to take a bit of "Burmantofts Ware" home with them and sit and look at it. It would last them a long time.' Each of the pieces was unique but all were unsigned and bear only the factory mark.

Numbers of small art potteries were established in the 1880s in various parts of England, notably in Devonshire and in the Midlands where there was a long-standing tradition of pottery-making. One of the most interesting of these, both for its origins and its connections with the Aesthetic Movement, was that of C. H. Brannam of Barnstaple in North Devon. In the seventeenth and eighteenth centuries Barnstaple had been an important pottery centre from which traditional domestic earthenware with slip and sgraffito decoration had been exported direct to America. By the mid nineteenth century Brannam's pottery was still making bread ovens and other large domestic wares on the site of its seventeenth-century forerunner. C. H. Brannam himself attended Barnstaple School of Art and later combined the new art teaching with the surviving craft tradition making art pottery. All the pieces

142

were executed in rich red earthenware coated with creamy slip and with some sgraffito decoration. In the late 1870s, under the influence of a visiting artist who admired the 'quaint' shapes, Brannam's work grew bolder and more original in form and the glazes became richer with the introduction of dark greens and browns. For many years C. H. Brannam designed, threw and decorated all the pieces himself and each piece was signed and dated. These decorative vases and jugs, each a unique piece with slight irregularities of form and decoration but informed by 'art' principles, were the embodiment of the ideas of the Arts and Crafts Movement and the complete antithesis of contemporary commercial production. Howell and James sold some of the first pieces but in 1882 Liberty became the sole London agents for Barum Ware, as it was called, and the association continued for some years forming a link with the Art Nouveau period. Later Brannam Pottery was marked as being made for Liberty and the traditional method of slip decoration seems to have been peculiarly well suited to the sinuous line demanded by Art Nouveau decoration.

Cast-iron seems, at first sight, to be a most unlikely material for an 'art' industry but the work of Barnard, Bishop and Barnard of the Norfolk Iron Works proved the contrary. Cast-iron was a popular material during the whole of the Victorian era, lavishly and skilfully used, but many of the industrial products were so conspicuously ill-designed that it was an obvious field for design reformers. Barnard, Bishop and Barnard produced both cast- and wrought-iron as well as wire goods of various kinds. Their work was of the highest technical quality and, unlike many other English exhibitors, at the 1851 Exhibition, their work was highly commended and they were later described as having initiated a renaissance of English metalwork. By the 1870s their work seems to have been universally praised in the most fulsome terms. The *Iron Age* of New York, writing of their exhibit at the Philadelphia Centennial, spoke of wonderful casting and brilliant design and, on the occasion of the Paris Exhibition two years later, another writer

Fig. 11 Cast-iron grate, designed by Thomas Jeckyll about 1876 and made by Barnard, Bishop & Barnard, Norwich. Reproduced from J. Moyr Smith, *Ornamental Interiors*.

said that 'by the exercise of a delicate fancy they may be said to have raised again the working of wrought-iron to its legitimate position amongst the Fine Arts.' This seems to have been a combination of the skill of the firm and the foresight of Alfred Barnard in employing Thomas Jeckyll as his designer. Thomas Jeckyll, a 'Japanese' designer, seems to have worked almost exclusively for Barnards during the last ten years of his life. Their mutual *pièce de résistance* was the Japanese exhibition pavilion (plate 66) but it was the ornamental and decorative stoves and grates which were the significant contribution to the Art Movement. They were well designed with pleasant and most effective ornament and they were launched on a long and successful career by the Prince of Wales. A stove, set with blue and gold art-painted tiles with a mantelpiece of American walnut, was the Prince's first personal purchase from the Paris Exhibition of 1878. The Prince of Wales also bought a pair of gates for Sandringham Park in Norfolk and another pair were bought for the then recently established Decorative Art Museum in Vienna. It is possible that Jeckyll's designs form another direct link with the later Art Nouveau as the sunflower railings for his Japanese pavilion bear a striking resemblance to one of the earliest designs for metal by the Spaniard, Antonio Gaudi (1852–1926). The Jeckyll design, dating from 1876, consists of repeated sunflowers with softly drooping leaves contained by firm vertical and horizontal lines (plate 116). They were the subject of one of the earliest experimental photographs published in the periodical *The British Architect*. The Gaudi railings for the Casa Vicens, designed in 1878, consist of repeated open palm leaves, extraordinarily similar in form to Jeckyll's sunflower petals.

In the late 1860s a small number of firms were producing well-designed goods for a small, informed public but as the Art Movement degenerated into a veritable mania for sunflowers, strange colours and terracotta ornaments, so almost any manufacturer with a feeling for publicity climbed on the artistic bandwaggon. On the credit side, it became much more general to employ designers for industrial products but by the mid eighteen-eighties only a few firms were maintaining the standards and the ideals which had originally inspired the Art Movement.

Chapter 8

THE FASHIONABLE AESTHETE

Aesthetic costume is a somewhat tantalizing subject of study. Unquestionably such clothing existed and was worn by many cultured women and their children and by some eccentric men in the late 1870s and early '80s but virtually no illustrations of it survive except in the form of caricature. One fashion journal was reported to have adopted what was called 'a startling innovation' in early 1881 in the form of large, full-length figure cartoons entitled 'Fashions for Art Folk' intended for ladies who chose to wear tasteful costumes of medieval suggestiveness, but this venture was clearly unusual. Fashionable, Paris-inspired dress of the same period was probably as elaborate in construction and as heavy to wear as at any time in the Victorian era. Bodices were tight-fitting, moulded to heavily-boned corsets, and skirts of the most complex construction consisted of layer upon layer of varied fabric and were further complicated by the addition of elaborate trimmings. Such garments called for individual professional dressmaking and considerable quantities of material so that there were obviously sound commercial reasons for the fashionable women's magazines, which had close ties with the retail trades, to confine their illustrations to these French fashions. The colour fashion plates published with each number all showed ladies and children in rather stiff attitudes in unbelievably elaborate garments. But the texts of these periodicals did occasionally give some hint of another, more individual approach to dress. In the summer of 1880, one Cicely, a reader of *The Queen*, was advised that she 'might embroider her bluish green art dress with peacock's feathers, the pattern carried from the shoulder down both sides of the front of the dress over the side darts as in the newest style of tennis aprons'. This lady and many others must have accepted this advice, for a writer in another periodical two years later reported that 'we have seen ladies wearing serge dresses embroidered with crewel wools but the effect was not happy'. Also in 1882 the aesthetic fashion was reported to have reversed the usual processes and passed across the Channel to Paris from London, as well as to New York, where 'women have begun to indulge in that chromatic misery, the green and yellow melancholy which is supposed to distinguish the Aesthetic habit of attire.'[1] It was an entirely new idea for London to influence Paris fashions, however briefly.

Despite the quips and criticism a very real change had come over the style of English fashionable dressing during the mid 1870s. Just as a variety

AN IMPARTIAL STATEMENT IN BLACK AND WHITE.

Fig. 12 'An Impartial Statement in Black and White' by George du Maurier from *Punch*, Volume 80, 1881. *Left*, Aesthetic Lady and Woman of Fashion. *Right*, Woman of Fashion and Aesthetic Lady.

of forms of architecture and interior decoration were socially acceptable, so two versions of fashionable dress existed side by side; one group of ladies favoured simple gowns, with flowing folds, while others wore the elaborate, stiffened, overweight fashions dictated by Paris and the modistes (fig. 12). These changes were produced by a number of factors working simultaneously, some artistic but possibly even more related to changing social conditions. Physical comfort had always been the last consideration involved in the design of fashionable female attire. Convenience, comfort and practicability were continuously sacrificed for the extremes dictated by each season's fashion whether it was currently to be under or over dressed. In the 1870s, however, a comfortable form of utilitarian dress became a necessity for some respectable young ladies who for the first time were beginning to work outside the home. Women were making great educational strides and were becoming nurses, teachers and social workers and even contemplating the professions of medicine and architecture, if a little tentatively. Stiffboned garments might appear elegant for social functions and their wearers might be prepared to put up with some discomfort for the sake of fashion but such garments were totally impractical for an active life outside the drawing-room. Another factor was increasing female participation in active sport, although only in a very mild form by modern standards. Thus by 1881 *The Queen*, in an editorial comment, came to the somewhat obvious conclusion that 'during recent years most girls have become convinced that tight stays and sleeves and tied-back skirts are incompatible with success in rowing or tennis'. A freer, looser form of sports costume was needed.

These pressing practical problems led to the establishment of The Rational Dress Association with the aim of reforming the taste of both the purchasing public and the designers and makers of clothing of all kinds. Their prospectus laid out the requirements of perfect dress and gave the names of the few firms willing to make dresses 'as far as possible in accordance with these requirements'. It is interesting to notice from the prospectus that one Parisian establishment had been recruited to the Rational Dress Movement. The requirements for perfect dress as enumerated were:

1. Freedom of movement.
2. Absence of pressure on any part of the body.
3. Not more weight than is necessary for warmth and both weight and warmth equally distributed.
4. Grace and beauty combined with comfort and convenience.
5. Not departing too conspicuously from the ordinary dress of the time.

This last cautionary provision marked the difference between artistic dress and the purely rational. Aesthetes were very much concerned with rational dress, just as they were concerned with the improved form of their dining-chairs, but their ultimate aim was beauty whereas the Rational Dress enthusiasts were primarily concerned with health, an understandable pre-occupation given the extremities to which the modiste had carried her clients in the mid 'seventies. This aim was reflected in the displays at the Association's exhibition held in 1883. According to the catalogue the exhibition included a few garments which were intended for formal occasions but quite the largest number were for sport of various kinds, such as swimming and bicycling, and there were even a number of discreet variations on the divided skirt. While this type of dress was commended for various practical virtues, as it was carefully disguised to give minimal offence, it did little to alter the appearance of the wearer. A change of shape of both dress and figure remained to be devised by the aesthetes.

The beauty with which they were primarily concerned was personified, in the first instance, by the flowing robes of the ladies in pre-Raphaelite painting. Mrs Haweis in her work on *The Art of Beauty* published in 1878 was even more specific and suggested that there should be a revival of the forms and colours of the years 1327–77. On the other hand, William Morris wrote, 'The period most worthy of reproduction is the ninth to the fourteenth century costume, perhaps those of 1250 being the most simple and elegant.'[2] Morris naturally took an interest in dress reform, one of 'the lesser arts of life', the increased beauty of which would make daily life more pleasurable. The recommended time span in itself gave a fairly free range of choice to the artistically inclined dressmaker but when the source of information on the period was confined to the few paintings available for study in public collections, and monochrome reproductions of others, the scope for invention was almost unlimited. The aim was to dress gracefully and to be in harmony with the domestic surroundings so that inevitably artistic fashions were governed by the current taste in art. Mrs Haweis wrote enthusiastically of the pre-Raphaelites: 'those dear and much abused painters whom it is still in some circles the fashion to decry who are the plain girl's best friends. They have taken all the neglected ones by the hand. All the ugly flowers, all the ugly buildings, all the ugly faces, they have shown us have a certain beauty of their own. Morris, Burne-Jones and others have made certain types of face and figure once literally hated actually the fashion. Red hair – once to say a woman had red hair was social assassination – is the rage. A pallid face with a protruding upper lip is highly esteemed – only dress after the pre-Raphaelite style and you will be astonished to find that so far from being an "ugly duck" you are a fully fledged swan.' The practical effect of the study of the pre-Raphaelites was to produce high-waisted flowing dresses with sleeves slightly puffed at the shoulders and always of soft fabrics in 'indescribable tints', tints dictated by current furnishing fashions and by the study of fourteenth-century painting.

The illustrated books of Kate Greenaway and Randolph Caldecott also provided models to be followed both by ladies and children of both sexes. The essential quality was that the wearer should appear as limp as possible and a contemporary account of an artistic 'at home' gave a graphic picture of the effects of this fashion. 'Two sad-eyed damsels with golden locks wore lank garments of white muslin, crumpled in a million creases; lilies in their hair and a long Annunciation lily carried in the hand. Another was dressed in a raiment of gold tissue with no vestige of waist or band; the two puffs on the shoulders gave the impression of being dilated by an immense sigh; the garment hung loosely about her long neck; tiger lilies were in her hair and crimson gloves reached midway up her arms.' In fact though some ladies looked a little strange, the mode was not inconsistent with grace and elegance, as is proved by Whistler's portrait of Mrs Leyland (plate 119), the wife of the patron of the Peacock Room. She was painted in soft pinks and greys and is shown in a gently-flowing, high-waisted muslin gown and standing on rush matting, the personification of the best of the Art Movement.

No doubt Mrs Leyland could afford the best advice and fabrics but one contemporary writer who actually favoured dress reform suggested that many artistic dresses deserved scorn and ridicule because the well-intentioned wearers lacked taste and their good ideas were clumsily executed. This criticism applied particularly to the use of embroidery on dress. 'Art' embroidery, 'a name recently introduced as a general term for all descriptions of needlework that spring from an application of knowledge of design and colouring, with skill in fitting and executing',[3] was usually worked in crewel wools in 'crewel' or 'Kensington' stitch, a form of irregular stem-stitch. While it could be attractive for furnishings, this type of work was far too coarse for clothing and the fact that truly artistic ladies were urged to make their own designs added a further hazard to the overall effect (fig. 13). Embroidery on a more modest scale seems to have been popular on the new tennis costumes and other art dresses were finished with broad bands of embroidery in silk on net, and by 1886 even shoemakers had adopted art embroidery. Ladies' boots with embroidered fronts were reported to be the rage, though not worked by the ladies themselves. Trade had stepped in at this stage and the work was commercially produced in Switzerland and Italy. Another innovation using embroidery was smocking on ladies' and children's dress. It was introduced as part of the 'Old English' revival, running parallel with similar tastes in architecture and decoration, but it was also favoured on health grounds particularly for children. A loose garment smocked at neck and wrist allowed more natural movement than more conventional clothing.

Fig. 13 'The Tidy Costume', from *Punch*, Volume 78, 1880.

93

Child of the Svn
Refvlgent
Svmmer comes

WITH EVERY GOOD WISH FOR THE NEW YEAR.

93 New Year Card, one of a set of prize-winning designs illustrating the seasons, by H. W. Batley for Hildesheimer & Faulkner, about 1880. *London, Victoria and Albert Museum.*

94 Christmas card by an unknown designer produced for Marcus Ward & Co. about 1880. *London, Victoria and Albert Museum.*

94

May you have a happy Christmas and many of them.

95

96

95   'The Little Red Girl',
greetings card designed by Kate
Greenaway for Marcus Ward &
Co. about 1878. *London, Victoria and
Albert Museum.*

96   Frontispiece from *A Day in a
Child's Life* by Kate Greenaway.
Engraved and printed by Edmund
Evans, 1881. *London, Victoria and
Albert Museum.*

97   'The Colonel Waltz' music
cover. A colour lithograph, 1881.
London, Victoria and Albert Museum.

To Edgar Bruce Esq.re

The Colonel

WALTZ

BY E. BUCALOSSI.

Price.... 4/-
Duet 4/-
Septett 1/-
Full Orchestra. 1/6
Military Band.

ENT. STA. HALL.

LONDON, HOPWOOD & CREW, 42, NEW BOND St. W.

STANNARD & SON.

As I was walking up the street,
  The steeple bells were ringing;
As I sat down at Mary's feet,
  The sweet, sweet birds were singing.

As I walked far into the world,
  I met a little fairy;
She plucked this flower, and, as it's sweet,
  I've brought it home for Mary.

99

THE GIRL IN YELLOW.

YELLOW on her head,
  Yellow on her feet,
Yellow on her dainty dress,
  On her girdle neat;
Yellow like a Daffodil,
  Blooming fresh and sweet.

Tell me, little maiden,
  How did you know
Yellow was the thing to wear;
  Who told you so?
A-fashioning your new dress—
  To whom did you go?

14

98 Illustration from *Aladdin or the Wonderful Lamp*, one of Walter Crane's Shilling Toy Books, published by George Routledge, 1874. *London, Victoria and Albert Museum.*

99 'The Girl in Yellow' from *Afternoon Tea* by Thomas Crane and J. G. Sowerby. Published by Frederick Warne, 1880. *London, Victoria and Albert Museum.*

100 Page from *Under the Window* by Kate Greenaway, published by Edmund Evans, 1879. *London, Victoria and Albert Museum.*

101   Three views of a painted porcelain teapot. The base is inscribed 'Fearful consequences through the laws of Natural Selection and Evolution of living up to one's teapot'. The design was registered 1881 and made by the Worcester Royal Porcelain Works, 1882. *Reproduced by Courtesy of the Trustees of the Dyson Perrins Museum Trust and the Worcester Royal Porcelain Works.*

102   Vase in the form of a pilgrim
bottle made in earthenware, with
painted decoration, designed by
H. Stacy Marks and made by
Minton's, dated 1877. *London,
Victoria and Albert Museum.*

103   Vase in the form of a pilgrim
bottle. Porcelain with moulded,
painted and gilt decoration,
modelled by James Hadley and
made by the Worcester Royal
Porcelain Company, 1872. *London,
Victoria and Albert Museum.*

104   Dish of earthenware painted
in colours by an unknown artist at
Minton's Art Pottery Studio,
Kensington Gore, about 1871–2.
Marked Minton's and signed
E. J. S. on the reverse.
G. W. Hawkins (Collection).

Fig. 14 'Valeria', a Liberty Art tea gown from a catalogue of about 1885. *London, Victoria and Albert Museum*

A painter whose work both reflected and influenced fashion was Albert Moore (1841–93), whose elegant ladies were usually shown in flowing white garments of some muslin-like fabric. In Moore's case the inspiration was not medieval painting but Greek sculpture, a source recommended by both artistic and rational fashion experts. Albert Moore's models were far more shapely and robust than those favoured by the pre-Raphaelites but their attitudes were suitably languid and their garments fell in graceful, soft folds (plate 60). Mrs Haweis suggested in *The Art of Beauty* that her readers would do well to spend some time studying both the larger pieces of Greek sculpture and the small Tanagra figures in the British Museum. The classical-style garments evolved from these studies in the early 1880s were cut loose and flowing but were worn over tight-fitting 'Princess' style dresses usually with very un-Greek puffed shoulder sleeves as favoured by the medievalists.

Since one of the main precepts of artistic dress was that it should blend with the new furnishings, and that the artistically dressed lady should be in harmony with her surroundings, furnishing colours and indeed furnishing fabrics were recommended for garments of all kinds. Artistic ladies of sensitivity shunned the garish, bright colours of the Paris fashion houses and adopted dull greens, peacock blue and dull, rich reds, or mellow amber-yellows. Mrs Haweis advised dull grass-green, with a slight yellow in it, as a picturesque colour for a woollen day dress, or sage green accompanied by deep lake, primrose or dull greenish-blue, and Liberty and Co. offered to their customers, 'Persian Pink, Venetian Red, Terracotta, Ochre-Yellow, Sapphire and Peacock Blue, Sage, Olive, Willow Green, Soft Brown and Drab'. Yet another 'authority' suggested the equally gloomy olive-green worn with turquoise for evening wear or for day dress almost any patterned fabric intended for furniture coverings or curtains. It was this fashion, no doubt, that prompted the printing on soft Indian silk of some of William Morris's designs for chintz. Gloomy as the recipe for aesthetic dress sounds, it was responsible for the introduction of some very lovely fabrics because the relative simplicity of line and shape demanded good pure fabrics which would drape well. Modish dress had become so extravagant of material that few could afford to be dressed, for instance, in pure silk which, in any case, lacked the body needed to support the artificial outlines demanded by fashion. The aesthetes used soft, pure silks, printed or plain, shantung or tusser silk for evening wear, and for day dress plain materials, such as Brown Holland, cream cotton with a linen stripe imported from Algeria, or printed cottons from India. By 1881 these fabrics could be obtained readily from 'any art warehouse', according to a writer in *The Queen* in that year.

First and foremost of these art warehouses was that of Liberty and Company which soon made a speciality of 'the particular class of oriental silks (properly termed Liberty silks) which are distinctly adapted for light clinging robes and draperies'. The dress fabric catalogue issued by the firm from which this quotation is taken, advertised a great range of Indian, Japanese and Chinese silks all commended to potential buyers for various artistic qualities. They were described as diaphanous, exquisite, suitable in every case for drapery and above all as aesthetic and artistic with the further commendation that such fabrics had been used in the stage costumes for

Patience, *The Colonel* and *The Cup* in which Ellen Terry had appeared. Liberty's were the first commercial firm to use the term 'Art Fabrics' as early as 1876 though others followed suit in the 1880s. 'The Aesthetic Gallery' was opened in Bond Street by a former Liberty partner, F. B. Goodyer, who specialized in English silks, cashmeres and velveteens and a Regent Street firm, A. Stephens and Company, set up as importers of Indian silks 'to promote the use of these fabrics for tasteful and artistic costume purposes'.

These soft materials were a great improvement on the dressed, stiffened silks and hard, glazed cottons which had been in general use in the earlier part of Queen Victoria's reign. Heavy fabrics had been so popular that silks had actually been chemically weighted to give a completely artificial appearance of richness comparable with the weighty and bulbous mid-Victorian furnishings. By demonstrating the success of his Oriental fabrics, Liberty was able to induce English manufacturers to produce lighter, softer materials, such as woven and printed silks, silk *crêpes* and gauzes, though the imports remained popular with the convinced aesthetes largely because of the circumstances of their manufacture. Wild silk, prepared and woven entirely by hand processes, with 'the consequent accidental irregularity in threads and weaving', conformed with the principles of the Arts and Crafts Movement based on the ideas of William Morris. Liberty fabrics were equally popular with the Rational Dress reformers and were included in their Exhibition in 1883 as playing 'an essentially prominent part in connection with Rational and Healthy Dress'. Their healthiness was guaranteed by their purity and comparative simplicity of production.

Following the success of the 'Art Fabrics' Liberty's opened a dress department in which artistic clothing was available ready made for ladies and children, for the most part designed by architects and painters (fig. 14). Some of the costumes were intended for fancy-dress and may well have been worn by the residents of Bedford Park for their Queen Anne soirées, but many were also intended for everyday wear. In 1884 a branch of Liberty's was opened in Paris also selling ready-made aesthetic clothes and the famous silks. It was these silks, the product of the English Aesthetic Movement, which so inspired the great Art Nouveau designer, Henri van de Velde. He first saw them in 1891 and described them as bringing '*une sorte de printemps*' new to the continental scene. By 1895 a writer in *The British Warehouseman* was able to claim with some satisfaction that Liberty costumes had become the centre of a Parisian social craze.

Despite well-meaning efforts, men's dress was singularly unaffected by all attempts at reform. It started with fewer disadvantages than the strangely malformed female attire and could hardly claim to be so unhealthy and detrimental to the health of the wearers. Even Oscar Wilde, known for eccentric costume, appeared by day in conventional clothing and merely donned knee-breeches and silk stockings for his public engagements, and the Rational Dress Association exhibited nothing more outlandish than gentlemen's bicycle dress. During his American lecture tour at Salt Lake City Oscar Wilde claimed, a little optimistically, that all England would soon dress as he did since 'the Prince of Wales and some of his friends have already pronounced in favour of the velvet coat, ruffles, knee-breeches and silk hose' but this may well have been merely colourful embroidery of his topic as there seems to be no other evidence to support this claim of royal patronage of dress reform. It seems probable that Wilde tactfully adjusted his dress ideas to his audience as on another American occasion he advised all men to dress like George Washington 'whose attire was noble and good' and after his visit to Colorado decided that the miners' large hats, loose corduroys and soft leather boots were ideal for male costume.

As with interior decoration, the strange extremes of fashion disappeared, as they always will, but the ultimate influence of the Aesthetic Movement on the textile trade and on fashion was beneficial. Colours were softer and more becoming and shapes were in some measure actually related to the female form.

Chapter 9

KATE GREENAWAY AND COMPANY

The eighteen-sixties and 'seventies saw a blossoming of art in the unexpected fields of children's illustrated books and of greetings cards and other printed ephemera. The two sorts of work were closely related as popular book illustrators also designed cards and both art forms were the direct outcome of the developing skills of the colour printer. English children had long been fortunate in the wealth and variety of their nursery literature but until the middle of the nineteenth century illustrations were usually small and tended to be subordinated to the text. The richly-coloured, well-designed picture book, accompanied by short verses or simple stories, was a product of the Aesthetic period and was produced in such quantity that by the early 1880s the contemporary child was said to be exceptionally well favoured in the matter of art. 'He may be said to be something of an art critic ere he leaves his cradle and an adept in style ere he sees fit to abandon long garments for short – his aesthetic opportunities are innumerable and the matter produced for the gratification of his pampered appetite is perhaps the daintiest ever seen.'[1] Children's reading matter had long been censored by parents and mentors on the ground of its moral content but the aesthetic parent was also concerned with the visual quality. Ellen Terry recorded in her memoirs the early training of her own two children, Edith and Gordon Craig, born in 1869 and 1871. 'They were allowed no rubbishy books but from the first Japanese prints lined the nursery walls and Walter Crane was their classic . . . this severe training proved so effective that when a doll dressed in a violent pink silk was given to Edy she said it was vulgar.'[2] Edith was some four or five years old at the time.

In some measure, this outburst of tasteful culture in the nursery may well have been due to a conscious attempt to instil right ideas about art but the credit is largely due to the enthusiasm and skill of one man. This was Edmund Evans (1826–1906), the engraver and colour printer, who was not only responsible for initiating and maintaining high standards of colour printing but was the first employer of such influential figures as Walter Crane and Kate Greenaway and he persuaded other established artists to work on coloured picture books.

After his apprenticeship as a wood engraver, Evans set up in business on his own account in 1851, engraving from the designs of a variety of artists and printing in black and white and colour from wood blocks. Apart from fine illustration, one of Evans's staple products was brightly-coloured book covers printed on yellow paper for the new railway bookstall market. It was as a designer of covers for sensational 'cheap railway novels' that Walter Crane (1845–1915) was first employed by Edmund Evans. The two men first met in 1863 when Crane was only eighteen and Evans recorded that he immediately recognized the young man's capabilities as a draughtsman and designer. In 1865, in association with the publisher Routledge, Evans embarked on a series of toy books. These were of a new, almost square format, with full-page illustrations in rich colours and the bold, vigorous design found in the best of contemporary popular or fairground art. It would appear that the subjects of these first books were suggested by Edmund Evans and a number of artists worked on them, including Walter Crane, but the actual illustrations were unsigned. The early toy book illustrations usually had solid, dark grounds with figures and animals in relief against them in vivid, plain colours, principally because the publishers were anxious to cater for the mid-Victorian taste for coarse colours and flamboyant design. After the proved success of the first toy books Walter Crane embarked on a series of children's books, some with his own text and some illustrating traditional fairy stories. He produced fifty complete books between 1865 and 1886 and continued with at least two a year almost until the end of the century. The designs were drawn direct on to the wood block by the artist who then added colour to the black proofs for the guidance of the block cutter and printer in the production of the finished illustrations. By 1869 or '70 Crane had evolved his personal and distinctive manner of illustration and was not only signing his work but his books were issued by the publishers in a separate category under the heading 'Walter Crane Toy Books'.

In his memoirs, Crane described the evolution of his style in which 'gradually more colours were used as the designs became more elaborate under various influences amongst which Japanese colour prints must be counted an important factor.'[3] First shown such prints in about 1868 by a naval officer who merely regarded them as curiosities, Crane immediately realized their relationship to his own woodcut illustrations and saw the further potentialities of the medium. A series of Crane's sixpenny and shilling picture books poured from the press of Edmund Evans during the early 'seventies, each bearing the stamp of the Aesthetic Movement in one way or another. The three bears, for example, grew sunflowers in their well-ordered garden and most of the characters in his stories used ebonized furniture and tasteful blue tiles in their homes. The covers of the shilling books carried a large version of the Japanese crane, adopted by Walter Crane as his signature just as Whistler had adopted the oriental butterfly. These covers, intended for the entertainment of children, were the epitome of the Art Movement, with their combination of assorted Japanese, Greek, Queen Anne and wilting aesthetic motifs, asymmetrically arranged. All the illustrations bore the mark of the influence of Japanese colour prints in their composition and colour while some, such as the colour plates for *Aladdin* in the shilling series, showed a sophisticated knowledge of oriental design with a rich profusion of Japanese motifs (plate 98).

Obviously Crane was familiar with the work of the pre-Raphaelites but at about the time that he embarked on his shilling books he first met Edward Burne-Jones. The impact of this meeting can be seen in many of the illustrations, particularly in those for *Princess Belle Etoile*, a fanciful tale in which Burne-Jones's figures were set in classical settings and ladies in aesthetic attitudes languished in Queen Anne interiors. A romanticized pre-Raphaelitism pervades the whole book but one illustration in particular derives directly from Burne-Jones's painting of 'St George and the Dragon', dating from some ten years earlier, with its graceful, willowy figure clad in armour encountering a dragon under Italianate trees (plate 108). A contemporary writer aptly commented on Mr Crane's decorative inventions as a combination of the medieval Hellas of Mr Burne-Jones and the medieval England of the architect of Bedford Park. Through the medium of his illustrations for children, Crane was one of the best publicists for the Aesthetic Movement to the principles of which he fully subscribed in the early days of his career. He was said to have refused to advise on the costumes and décor for *Patience* as he was reluctant to be involved in guying his own beliefs. Crane was well aware of his influence, even outside the nursery, as he recorded that it was his practice to put into the illustrations any sort of detail that interested him and to make use of any opportunity to demonstrate his ideas on furniture and decoration.[4] In fact this policy led directly to a number of commissions for interior decoration and in 1875 to his earliest wallpaper designs produced for Jeffrey and Company. This first design was for a nursery paper incorporating such nursery rhyme figures as Bo Peep and the Queen of Hearts and was followed by others, 'Little Queen Anne' and 'The Sleeping Beauty' (plate 14).

In addition to his book illustrations, Walter Crane designed greetings cards for the firm of art publishers, Marcus Ward, of which his brother Thomas, also a competent illustrator, was the art director. This was a Belfast-based firm, initially concerned with playing cards, which entered the greetings card business in about 1870 and eventually controlled much of the market, becoming a significant influence on the production of other art publishers. Christmas and other greetings cards had only come into general use in the middle of the nineteenth century and most of them were imported from the German states or France. Charming though they may appear today their florid style made them an obvious target for aesthetic reform. At the time of the Franco-Prussian war in 1870 when Paris was temporarily closed to trade, Marcus Ward and Company seized their opportunity and inaugurated a profitable venture into the greetings card market with such immediate success that by Christmas of the same year it could be said that 'their merest trifles are sound Art-teachers and they circulate nothing that endangers a true and pure taste for that which is excellent in art.'[5] This applied to the text of Marcus Ward's greetings as well as the designs. For example, one typical New Year card expressed the wish that the fairest forms of Art and Nature should surround the recipient in the coming year.

With Thomas Crane as their art editor Marcus Ward and Company employed numbers of artists subscribing to aesthetic ideas. Some were anonymous (plate 94) but others were already known for their work in other fields of aesthetic endeavour, such as H. Stacy Marks (plate 102) and J. Moyr Smith (plate 113) known for the painted panels on ebonized furniture or tile designs. Their Christmas card subjects were scenes of Old English revelry in which yule logs were carried or rich meals were prepared by worthy citizens clad in medieval dress. Basically they showed respectable Victorian families transposed into an Old English setting. Thomas Crane himself designed floral cards with ornamental borders incorporating aesthetic motifs as well as similar designs for some of the children's books which Marcus Ward began to publish in 1873. Two of these books, the joint work of Thomas Crane, his cousin Ellen Houghton and another artist, J. G. Sowerby, are some of the most charming publications of the period. Entitled *At Home* and *Abroad* they were published by Marcus Ward and Company in 1881 and 1882 respectively on the crest of the Art Movement. They record the home life in London and the travels in France of a family of children who lived in a Queen Anne house and dressed in shades of green, peacock blue and sepia that would have done credit to Mrs Haweis and other arbiters of taste. Each page of verse is surrounded by charming and appropriate borders designed, as were the endpapers, by Thomas Crane. The actual illustrations and figures are by Ellen Houghton and John Sowerby (see also plate 111).

As the popularity of artistic greetings cards grew other publishers entered the field, employing a variety of artists and even promoting competitions to find suitable designs for an ever-increasing range of occasional greetings. Emphasis was upon quality of design and printing rather than on illustration of the season or event celebrated so that, for instance, there were virtually no art cards with any religious significance. Asymmetry and aesthetic colour became the hallmarks of tasteful greeting for every occasion. Wilting aesthetes with sunflowers and teapots were sent at Christmas time (plate 109) and one publisher specialized in semi-nude nymphs in vaguely classical seaside settings, based on watercolours by W. S. Coleman (plate 106). H. W. Batley, a dedicated aesthete, better known amongst his contemporaries as an interior decorator and furniture designer, won a greetings card competition with a most original and charming group of cards illustrating the seasons (plate 93). Amateurs designed cards, just as they painted on pottery or designed embroidery, and their works were occasionally selected for actual publication. The standard of work seems to have been reasonably high and a critic commenting in the *Magazine of Art* on an exhibition of Christmas cards held in a London gallery in 1881, wrote of the proof given by the exhibits of the recent general spread of better taste in the daily life of the English. However he regretted that some of the designs were 'flaccid illustrations from Tennyson' and that still more were pale imitations of the work of Kate Greenaway. While less influential in the long term than, for example, the work of Walter Crane, Kate Greenaway's personal style was imitated more or less successfully by many of her contemporaries.

Kate Greenaway (1846–1901) began her career as an artist in about 1871 with Christmas card designs for Marcus Ward in which little girls in high-waisted frocks and sunbonnets skipped gaily surrounded by delicate garlands of flowers (plate 95). At about the same time she was employed on some bold and more conventional woodcut designs for *Aunt Louisa's Toy Books* published by Frederick Warne, but these were published anonymously and were quite unlike her later work. Kate Greenaway's father was an engraver and an acquaintance of Edmund Evans to whom he showed a group of his daughter's drawings and simple nonsense verses. Evans was so struck by their quality that he persuaded Routledge to publish the collection with the title *Under the Window* and on his own initiative printed a first edition of 20,000 copies. He was convinced that the charm, quaintness and originality of the drawings would make the book a popular success. His confidence proved well-founded for the first edition issued in 1878 sold out almost immediately and Kate Greenaway's reputation was established not only in England but also in America (plate 100). Following this success, she illustrated numbers of books in her own quaint style, often supplying her own brief text and sometimes co-operating with other authors. Her prettily-dressed little boys and girls played innocent games, gathered flowers or took afternoon tea in idyllic rural settings strongly reminiscent of the villages of Sussex and Kent whose red brick cottages had already inspired aesthetic architects. The children were dressed in an entirely original style which owed something to late eighteenth- and nineteenth-century children's fashions but was essentially 'Kate Greenaway', a style so admired that budding aesthetes were soon dressed to match the books, a unique achievement for a book illustrator. It was recorded that the clever Miss Greenaway actually made costumes to her own designs for her child models. Her illustrations were always in subdued tones with an extensive use of soft yellows and greens and Evans excelled himself in the skill with which he reproduced the delicate designs (plate 96). Charming as the illustrations were they were nonetheless pervaded by an extraordinary melancholy typical of the Aesthetic Movement. The children all have a subdued and somewhat depressed air even when accompanying gay verses but the designs were so in keeping with the mood of the times that they provoked a rush of imitators.

Typical of the best of these were the greetings cards of Mrs Koberwein Terrell but it is of some interest that no less than nineteen lithographically-printed colours were needed for the reproduction of her pictures to achieve a standard of printing comparable to Edmund Evans's wood engravings (plate 110). Evans himself refused to print one book offered to him by a Kate Greenaway imitator. This was *Afternoon Tea*, drawn and written by J. G. Sowerby and eventually printed by some half-dozen different printers and published by Frederick Warne in 1880 (plate 99). It is a pleasant book but the illustrations are neither as well drawn nor as well printed as in the real Kate Greenaway books, and it is easy to see how her personal reputation eventually suffered through the association of her name with the work of her imitators.

As a member of the family glass manufacturing firm of Sowerby of Gateshead, J. G. Sowerby (working 1876–1914) was a successful glass designer in his own right. The firm was an old-established one and it can be assumed that it was due to the influence of John Sowerby that their art glass was introduced in the mid 1870s. They were far in advance of other glass

105

105   Tile, designed by Kate
Greenaway, made of earthenware,
transfer printed in colours and
made by T. & R. Boote,
Birmingham, 1883. *London,
Victoria and Albert Museum.*

They would gaze upon a lily, s
    utterably utter,"
With eyes distended wide as
    blossom they'd devour;
'Twas easy to believe they had
    quished bread and butter,
And really lived on nothing mo
    stantial than a flower.

106   Original design for a
greetings card for Messrs de la Rue
by William Coleman, about 1880.
London, Victoria and Albert Museum.

107   Page from *The Decorative
Sisters*, a 'Modern Ballad' by
Josephine Pollard, illustrated by
Walter Satterlee and published in
New York, 1882. *London, Victoria
and Albert Museum.*

108

108   Illustration from *Princess
Belle Etoile*, one of Walter Crane's
Shilling Toy Books, published by
George Routledge, 1874. *London,
Victoria and Albert Museum.*

MAY·YOU·HAVE·A·QUITE·TOO·HAPPY·TIME·

109

WISHING YOU AN UTTERLY CHARMING T

109   Christmas cards designed by
Albert Ludovici Junior, 1881.
London, Victoria and Albert Museum.

110 Christmas card from a
prize-winning design by Mrs
Georgina Koberwein Terrell,
printed by Raphael Tuck & Sons in
nineteen colours, about 1880.
London, Victoria and Albert Museum.

110

RAPHAEL TUCK & SONS.   ALL CHRISTMASTIDE MAY JOY ABIDE!   PRIZE DESIGN   LONDON

111 'The Lowther Arcade' from
London Town by Thomas Crane and
Ellen Houghton, published by
Marcus Ward, 1883. *London,
Victoria and Albert Museum.*

111

112

112   Illustration from *A Frog He
Would a-Wooing Go*, one of
Randolph Caldecott's picture
books printed by Edmund Evans
about 1878. *London, Victoria and
Albert Museum.*

113

'The Four Seasons'; tiles designed by J. Moyr Smith and made by Minton's, about 1880. *Washington, Smithsonian Institute.*

manufacturers of the day in design and their catalogues were full of original ideas for opaque pressed glass, or what Sowerby's called 'vitro porcelain', incorporating aesthetic and Japanese motifs (plates 80, 81). Significantly a number of their smaller pieces were decorated with friezes of Kate Greenaway-type children and were first made in 1878, the year of publication of *Under the Window*.

The third of the distinguished illustrators who worked with Edmund Evans was Randolph Caldecott (1846–86). His background was entirely different from that of Walter Crane and Kate Greenaway. Born in Manchester, he moved to London in 1872 and immediately came under the influence of the Aesthetic Movement. Following a visit to the International Exhibition in Vienna in 1873 he began to paint Japanese-inspired compositions and ventured into the field of interior decoration while at the same time learning modelling from the French sculptor, Jules Dalou, then resident in Chelsea. While pursuing these varied interests his main source of revenue would seem to have been book illustration. It was his pen drawings, engraved on wood as illustrations to *Old Christmas* and *Bracebridge Hall* by Washington Irving, that so impressed Edmund Evans that he asked Caldecott to do some shilling toy books. The first two, *The House that Jack built* and *John Gilpin*, were issued by Routledge in 1878, a vintage year for children's books. These were followed by fourteen others before Caldecott's early death in 1886. All printed by Edmund Evans in ever-increasing editions, they were beautiful productions, skilfully printed in delicate watercolour-like tints. Caldecott was not only a skilful draughtsman but a most entertaining story-teller, even within the framework of each illustration, and his work is quite untouched by the melancholy of his contemporaries though bearing many of the trade marks of the Art Movement. One of his most attractive books was *A Frog he would a-Wooing go* (plate 112) in which the animal participants, though living in one of the late eighteenth-century houses which passed for Queen Anne and sitting on Morris Sussex chairs, are given scale by the occasional interpolation of human observers. Miss Mouse must be presumed to have subscribed to aesthetic views as her simple classic fireplace was ornamented with peacock feathers.

Caldecott's illustrations form an interesting link between the English Art Movement and the continental arts of the latter part of the century. It was Caldecott's practice to spend holidays in the Breton village of Pont Aven where it seems possible that he met Gauguin. There is a striking similarity between Caldecott's little terracotta figures of Breton peasants, made after his work with Dalou, and Gauguin's early pottery, both dating from the mid 'eighties. In addition the Scottish painter, A. S. Hartrick, also a frequenter of the Breton artists' colony, recorded that Gauguin possessed some of Caldecott's coloured books. On one occasion Gauguin 'produced one in which some geese were depicted in the artist's characteristic way. These he praised, extravagantly', and commented on the true spirit of the drawing.[6] It may well have been due to Gauguin's enthusiasm that Crane's and Caldecott's illustrated children's books were included, together with his own ceramics, in one of the first Continental Arts and Crafts exhibitions held in Belgium in 1891.

Regrettably the standard of design and production set by Edmund Evans in his work was not maintained by other printers and publishers but it is a measure of the quality of the artistic picture books of the 'seventies and 'eighties that many of them have remained continuously in print for almost a century.

Chapter 10

QUEEN ANNE TO ART NOUVEAU

'Tonight there passes away the most memorable quarter of a century in the annals of Art which this country has known since the brilliant periods of the Middle Ages.'[1] Thus wrote the editor of *The British Architect* on New Year's Eve 1875, voicing the new-found self-confidence and excitement about the future of English art that was felt by so many architects, designers and artists. The statement was obviously an extravagant evaluation of all but a few of the actual products of the period but, nonetheless, those twenty-five years did contain the germ of much that was to be of importance later in the century, both in England and on the Continent. It was the period that saw the rise of the pre-Raphaelites, the introduction of William Morris's first designs, of a new style of architecture, of Japanese influence, and with all this the Aesthetic Movement. These last two, coupled with the spread of the ideas of Ruskin and Morris and the consequent turning to nature as a source of inspiration, led directly to what is now known as Art Nouveau. It is significant that in England the style was first known as New Art as it was seen as a progression from the earlier Art Movement.

The relationship between the Art Nouveau and its English forerunner is intricate and complex and, while the two movements had many similarities, their differences are equally marked. The Aesthetic Movement was a self-conscious revival or renaissance of the decorative arts and, as it was in part inspired by a certain social consciousness, it was essentially missionary. Artists and designers worked simultaneously to improve the taste of their public, intending by this method to improve the actual conditions of life. As the sun gives colour to flowers so art gives colour to life, as one contemporary artist expressed it. The aestheticism of the 1870s and the Arts and Crafts Movement of the 1880s inspired designers with ideals and produced a way of working and an attitude to life rather than a style. There were similarities of form and some common decorative motifs, trade marks as it were, such as the lily and the sunflower, but the relationship between an ebonized sideboard, a Doulton Art pot and a Morris wallpaper is not immediately apparent on purely stylistic grounds.

On the other hand international Art Nouveau, which came to full and brief flower in the later 1890s, is immediately recognizable, identified by the sinuous organic line and sensuous curves of both form and ornament. As will be seen later, it was generally accepted that this evolved from the 'sentimental passion for a vegetable fashion' mocked by Gilbert and Sullivan and found in the English design of the 'seventies and even earlier. Like Aestheticism before it, Art Nouveau was a movement of pure individualism but this time there were no missionaries. The concept of Art for Art's sake was wholly accepted and artists and designers worked with an almost complete disregard for their public. In addition, the decorative arts adopted the conscious search for decadence which had been present in European literature, particularly in France and Belgium, during much of the second half of the nineteenth century. There were 'many young men eager for the distinction of decay'. The concept of decadence was in part related to the symbolism of the dying century. *Evergreen*, one of the many short-lived periodicals of the 1890s, gave this explanation saying that artists were seeking 'only to link the autumn of our age with an approaching spring and pass through decadence towards Renaissance' and that decadence was a mere 'autumn sickness and one of rapid growth and adolescence'. The intention was to create something new and fresh for the new century and the English Art Movement with its very different aims, and the writings of William Morris and some of his contemporaries, set the mood of all the work if not necessarily establishing its form. 'No more museum-inspired work; no more scruples about styles; no more dry as dust stock patterns . . . but instead designs by living men for living men. We must clothe modern ideas in modern dress, adorn our design with living fancy and rise to the height of our knowledge and capacity.' These are the words not of some wild revolutionary of the 'nineties but of a follower of William Morris, the architect and designer J. D. Sedding. As a good pupil of Ruskin and Morris, Sedding recommended an alternative source of inspiration. 'Drop this wearisome translation of old styles and translate nature instead.' It is this translation of nature in one form or another that provides the visual link between the Aesthetic Movement and Art Nouveau. There is obviously a danger in assuming that a similarity of shape or design necessarily implies a common source or influence but, though the relationship between an early Morris wallpaper and the wild floral swirls of the eighteen-nineties may not be immediately apparent, the one is a direct descendant of the other.

'The Daisy' wallpaper which was designed by Morris for the 1862 Exhibition was the trend-setter of its day. An obvious repeating pattern with the simplest of flowers directly observed as its motif, it was in marked contrast to the exuberant papers popular with the trade at the time. The principle of the strong main motif derived from nature, with a more rigid subsidiary one, giving an underlying flatness and stability, was one that was used later by Morris himself in more complex designs and by most English designers of the latter part of the century. It can be seen in the simple floral papers of Lewis F. Day (plate 10), the work of Walter Crane and many others. Even the Japanese-inspired work of E. W. Godwin contains the same elements used with increasing freedom. 'The Peacock' paper designed in 1873 consists of two motifs, the peacock and the textured background, both taken directly from Japanese badge or heraldic designs merely enlarged and simplified (plate 73). However the floral design intended for use with 'The Peacock' though Japanese in inspiration, is not based on any specific model.

It has the stability of a fairly rigid ground but the natural forms flow freely. This free-flowing quality which has been called Proto-Art Nouveau was characteristic of much of the English design of the 'seventies. An embroidery designed by Morris at the height of the aesthetic fashion (plate 27), with its sunflowers peeping from behind undulating leaf forms, is typical of the best of Morris's flat pattern design and clearly contains all the seeds of Art Nouveau. The same tendencies can be seen in an anonymously-designed wallpaper (plate 74). This and the embroidery both date from 1877, fully twenty years before the new movement acquired its continental name.

The strange fact is that having in effect created Art Nouveau in the 1870s England abandoned and even shunned the style once it had become a fashion. Lewis F. Day's simple sunflowers and sprays of apple blossom (plate 10) evolved into naturally-swaying forms such as those of the printed velveteen of about 1890 (plate 121). It is significant that this is one of the many examples of Day's work chosen for illustration in 1892 in one of the first German publications dealing with what were then called the modern naturalistic styles.[2] The first volume of this periodic survey contains dozens of designs by Morris, Lewis F. Day and Walter Crane, most of them originally published at least ten years earlier. Walter Crane's peacocks, swans and lilies led quite naturally to what he himself called 'that strange decorative disease known as L'Art Nouveau'. While Crane's much illustrated and exhibited work was an acknowledged source of inspiration for the continental movement he was one of the most violent critics of its 'wild and whirligig squirms', apparently quite unable to see the logical extension of his own work and that of his English contemporaries. Apart from the surviving visual evidence there seems to have been fairly general contemporary agreement that Art Nouveau had well-established roots in England. Alfredo Melani, the Italian critic, writing in 1902 on the occasion of the opening of the first International Exhibition of Modern Decorative Art, felt that there would inevitably be thousands of English visitors, as the exhibition was the greatest expression of 'the modern aesthetic movement the first ideas of which really originated in England'.

Art Nouveau was originally the name of a shop in Paris established in 1896 by Samuel Bing for the display and sale of work by all those with a 'distinct personal perception whose designs were not re-incarnations of the past'. A French visitor to Bing's shop in Paris said that she was able to see the influence of Morris and Burne-Jones in all the work there and an English critic in *The Art Journal* of 1897 felt so certain of his English superiority that he asserted that 'to the Parisian the decoration applied to the rooms might appear new but for those who know the English style now in vogue curiosity is certainly less.' This anonymous writer went so far as to accuse van de Velde of copying Mr Walter Crane but of rendering his ideas without charm.

There was in fact some foundation for this accusation as, of all the artists whose names were associated with Art Nouveau, it was van de Velde (1863–1957) who paid the most whole-hearted tribute to his English masters, specifically to the ideas of Ruskin and Morris and the designs of Walter Crane. Though he had come into contact with English design a year or two earlier, van de Velde first wrote of his new enthusiasm in the French periodical *L'Art Moderne* in 1893. Significantly he used the English language for the title, calling his article 'Artistic Wallpapers'. English art wallpapers had been shown in Paris at the International Exhibition of 1889 and were subsequently imported into Belgium together with Liberty textiles and other examples of artistic English household goods. In addition Walter Crane's illustrated children's books were amongst the English contributions to the 1891 salon of *Les Vingt*, the *avant-garde* group of Belgian sculptors and painters. This was the first occasion on which decorative arts were shown in what had previously been a fine art exhibition and it was at about this time that van de Velde himself abandoned his career as a painter and began to design furniture, textiles, metalwork and eventually architecture. First he set himself the task of becoming thoroughly familiar with what he described as the recent revival of handicrafts in England and to this end it seems likely that he visited the third annual exhibition of the Arts and Crafts Exhibition Society held in London in 1893, as he quoted extensively in the wallpaper article, from Crane's catalogue foreword. The Society, whose original name had been 'The Combined Arts', embodied all van de Velde's ideas for reform in the decorative arts and its president was Walter Crane. After acknowledging the debt of the Arts and Crafts Movement both in England and abroad to William Morris, van de Velde went on to list almost all the contemporary English pattern designers including Lewis Day, Sedding and C. F. A. Voysey but his final conclusion was that Walter Crane triumphed over all the others by virtue of the rhythmic vegetation in his designs and *'les lignes de très spéciale souplesse'*. These of course were the very qualities which marked the most extreme expression of continental Art Nouveau and it is obvious from van de Velde's detailed analysis of each of Crane's designs that these contributed significantly to his own decorative work in its formative stage in the early 1890s.

Curiously Crane was not alone in his aversion to Art Nouveau. Almost all the English designers whose work provided the basis for later developments in Belgium, France and, in particular, in Austria and Germany, turned from Art Nouveau around the end of the century almost with revulsion, adopting a national puritan view in the face of what they regarded as an unwholesome foreign disease.

There seems to have been only one artist whose career coincided at each stage with the apparently logical developments from the Art Movement of the 1880s, through Arts and Crafts to Art Nouveau and the twentieth century. This was the American Louis Comfort Tiffany (1848–1933). Trained as a painter, he continued painting throughout his life unlike others, such as van de Velde who made a complete break with fine art under the influence of the Arts and Crafts Movement. In the late '60s and early '70s Tiffany worked in Paris and visited North Africa and Palestine, experiences which affected his later decorative work. One of the main factors in Tiffany's diversion from fine to applied art was his association with Edward C. Moore, chief silver designer to the family firm of Tiffany and Company, and friend of Samuel Bing. Before opening his famous Art Nouveau shop Bing was a collector of oriental art, as was Moore, whose particular enthusiasm was near-Eastern glass. Under his guidance Tiffany embarked on his own collection of Japanese objects. An additional influence was that of Donald G. Mitchell, a relative of Tiffany who was actively engaged in the Art Movement and in this capacity was chairman of the judges of Decorative Arts at the Philadelphia Centennial Exhibition. There was a considerable quantity of English art work shown at Philadelphia and in his report of the exhibition Mitchell singled out for commendation to his countrymen the work of Walter Crane. Crane, Morris and Burne-Jones were also the inspiration behind the first of Tiffany's practical ventures into the decorative arts. He designed, advised and helped the New York Society of Decorative Art, a body principally concerned with art embroidery founded by Mrs Candace Wheeler in 1878 in imitation of the Royal School of Art Needlework in South Kensington.

Tiffany's next step in 1879 was to start his own firm, Associated Artists, to undertake complete interior design projects. At this stage the work of the firm was remarkably similar to that of English interior designers such as W. H. Batley, Lewis F. Day and Thomas Jeckyll, and Tiffany is known to have seen the Godwin and Whistler exhibit at the Paris Exhibition of 1878. The firm's first really original work was the decoration of the Veterans' Room of the Seventh Regiment Armory in New York completed in 1880, a rich, dark room in which Tiffany improbably but successfully combined motifs from Celtic, Moorish and medieval art into a completely unified

Fig. 15 Part of the decoration of the Lyceum Theatre, New York, designed by Louis C. Tiffany, 1884, from a contemporary drawing illustrated in *The Magazine of Art*.

scheme of decoration. The ceiling was of dark wood covered with a stencilled decoration in silver, a favourite motif at this date which was repeated in the interior of the Lyceum Theatre, New York, decorated by Tiffany in 1884. An English critic, writing in the *Magazine of Art* in the same year, was able to find Turkish, Arabian and even what he described as Louis Quinze details in the scheme but could also see the unifying effect of the personal quality of Tiffany's design in an ensemble rich with silver and gold stencilling and 'glittering with streams of silver paint'. The critic of the *New York Morning Journal*, obviously surprised by the originality of the design, commented that 'it belongs to no school unless the ultra aesthetic school of Wilde'.

Tiffany had used stained glass and had experimented with glass tiles in his earliest interiors but in the latter part of 1885 he established another firm, the Tiffany Glass Company, initially concerned exclusively with the production of stained-glass windows. It was this venture that provided the link between Tiffany's work and the European Art Nouveau Movement. When he visited Paris for the International Exhibition of 1889, Tiffany approached Bing with his ideas for stained glass and the two formed a lasting association which derived from their mutual admiration for William Morris and the Arts and Crafts Movement and which was to become a major influence on Art Nouveau. Early in the 1890s Tiffany began his experiments with blown glass, and the first pieces of iridescent Favrile glass were sold by Bing in his Art Nouveau establishment in Paris. Curiously the intention behind these experiments with blown glass was a desire to provide household objects of everyday use which would enrich by their beauty the lives of average American citizens. However from this worthy missionary aim evolved some of the most precious, elegant, exquisite and totally impractical products of Art Nouveau, sought by European collectors and museums and far beyond the pocket of the average householder. Thus objects personifying Art Nouveau were produced for the same reasons that had inspired the earlier aesthetes and under craft conditions based on the English Arts and Crafts Movement.

Tiffany's career demonstrates the extent to which Art Nouveau, of which he was one of the most distinguished exponents, was rooted in the innovations of the 1860s. Despite their obvious differences of both form and intention, the two linked movements proved to be equally important and related parts of the transition between the eclectic historicism of the early nineteenth century and the disciplined and purposeful style of the Modern Movement of the twentieth century.

114   Sunflower in wrought iron,
designed by Thomas Jeckyll and
made by Barnard, Bishop &
Barnard, Norwich, 1876. *London,
Victoria and Albert Museum.*

Overleaf

115   Pencil drawing of a bracket
panel for the Japanese Pavilion by
Thomas Jeckyll, 1876. *London,
Victoria and Albert Museum.*

116   Pencil drawing of a bracket
panel for the Japanese Pavilion by
Thomas Jeckyll, 1876. *London,
Victoria and Albert Museum.*

117

117 Detail from 'Private View of
the Royal Academy, 1881' by
W. P. Frith (1819–1909). Oil on
canvas, 1881. The group includes
portraits of many well-known
figures of the day: Oscar Wilde
and Ellen Terry with Gordon
Craig. *Major A. C. R. Pope.*

118 'Love's Altar' by Walter
Crane, signed with his monogram
and dated 1870. Oil on canvas.
*Walthamstow, William Morris
Gallery.*

I

119 'Symphony in Flesh Colour
and Pink'; portrait of Mrs F. R.
Leyland by J. M. Whistler,
1872–3. Oil on canvas. *New York,
Frick Collection.*

120   Drawing of a panel of
stained glass from the Prince of
Wales's Pavilion at the Paris
Exhibition of 1878, made by
J. Powell & Sons, Whitefriars.

Notes

CHAPTER I   Introduction

1 *Furniture Gazette*, vol. v, 1876, p. 76.   2 William Morris, *Collected Works*, vol. 23, p. 154. 'Art, Wealth and Riches'.   3 Walter Hamilton, *The Aesthetic Movement in England*, 1882, p. vii.   4 M. Digby Wyatt, *Reports on the Exhibitions*, H.M.S.O., 1856.   5 *The Art Manufactures of Birmingham & the Midland Counties*, Birmingham, 1862. 6 *Punch*, 1879.   7 Roger Fry, *Vision and Design*, London, 1920, p. 27. 'The Ottoman and the Whatnot'.

CHAPTER III   The Aesthetic Interior

1 C. L. Eastlake, *Hints on Household Taste*, London, 1872, p. 60.   2 *Ibid.*, p. 92.   3 Harriett Prescott Spofford, *Art Decoration Applied to Furniture*, New York, 1878.   4 Anon., *Artistic Homes*, London, about 1880, p. 75.   5 *The Artist*, vol. 1, 1880, p. 345.   6 *The Builder*, vol. XLI, 1881, p. 196.   7 J. Moyr Smith, *Ornamental Interiors*, 1887, p. 82.   8 Mrs H. R. Haweis, *The Art of Beauty*, London, 1878, p. 232.   9 J. Forbes-Robertson, *A Player under Three Reigns*, London, 1925, p. 66.   10 *The Architect*, Aug., 1876, p. 73.   11 H. W. Batley, *A Series of Studies for Domestic Furniture and Decoration*, London, 1883.   12 Harry Quilter, 'Fashion and Art or Spots on the Sunflower', 1881, reprinted in *Opinion on Men, Women and Things*, London, 1909.

CHAPTER V   Oscar Wilde and America

1 'Swinburne and Water', *Punch*, vol. 81, 1881, p. 26.   2 Oscar Wilde, *The English Renaissance of Art*, Essays and Lectures, 6th edition, 1928, p. 154.   3 *British Architect*, vol. XVIII, 1882, p. 534.   4 Oscar Wilde, *Art and the Handicraftsman*, Essays & Lectures, 6th edition, 1928, p. 195.   5 William Morris, *The Beauty of Life*, Works, vol. XXII, p. 77. 6 Walter Hamilton, *The Aesthetic Movement in England*, 2nd edition, 1882, p. 100.   7 *Punch*, vol. 82, 1882, p. 14.

CHAPTER VI   Satire and Comment

1 *Punch*, vol. 72, 1877, 'Modern Aesthetics', p. 51.   2 *Punch*, vol. 78, 1880, 'A Love Agony', p. 254.   3 *Punch*, vol. 77, 1880, p. 303.   4 *Punch*, vol. 81, 1881, p. 241.   5 *Punch*, vol. 81, 1881, p. 154.   6 *British Architect*, vol. xv, 1881, p. 379.   7 *British Architect*, vol. XVIII, 1882, p. 534.

CHAPTER VII   'Art' Industry

1 *Studio*, vol. xv, 1899, pp. 104–14.   2 *The Artist*, vol. II, 1881, p. 88.   3 *The Paris Exhibition of 1878*; An illustrated Weekly Review, Christmas, 1878, p. 634.   4 *Art Journal*, vol. IX, 1870, p. 381.

CHAPTER VIII   The Fashionable Aesthete

1 *The Magazine of Art*, vol. v, 1882, p. xii.   2 William Morris, 'The Lesser Arts of Life', lecture delivered in support of the Society for the Protection of Ancient Buildings. 3 Caulfeild and Saward, *Dictionary of Needlework*, 1882.

CHAPTER IX   Kate Greenaway and Company

1 'Art in the Nursery', *The Magazine of Art*, vol. VI, 1883, p. 127.   2 Ellen Terry, *Memoirs*, London, 1933, p. 66.   3 Walter Crane, *An Artist's Reminiscences*, London, 1907, p. 74. 4 *Ibid.*, p. 156.   5 *Art Journal*, vol. IX, 1870, p. 381.   6 A. S. Hartrick, *A Painter's Pilgrimage*, Cambridge, 1939.

CHAPTER X   Queen Anne to Art Nouveau

1 *British Architect*, vol. LV, 1875, p. 361.   2 Ed. Julius Hoffman Jnr., *Für das Kunstgewerbe*, Stuttgart Bilderschatz, 1892.

121   Printed velveteen designed by Lewis F. Day, 1890. *London, Victoria and Albert Museum.*

Selected Bibliography

Anon., *Artistic Homes*. London, 1880.

Alford, Lady Marion, *Needlework as Art*. London, 1886.

Batley, H. W., *A Series of Studies for Domestic Furniture and Decoration*. London, 1883.

Baker, Lady, *The Bedroom and the Boudoir*. London, 1878.

Carr, Mrs J. Comyns, *Reminiscences*. London, about 1920.

Conway, Moncure Daniel, *Travels in South Kensington*. London, 1882.

Cook, Clarence, *The House Beautiful*. New York, 1878.

Crane, Lucy, *Art and the Formation of Taste*. London, 1882.

Crane, Walter, *An Artist's Reminiscences*. London, 1907.

Crane, Walter, *William Morris to Whistler*. London, 1911.

Day, Lewis F., *Everyday Art. Short Essays on the Arts Not-Fine*. London, 1882.

Eastlake, C. L., *Hints on Household Taste*. London, 1867.

Edis, R. W., *Decoration and Furniture of Town Houses*. London, 1881.

Garrett, R. & A., *House Decoration*. London, 1876.

Hamilton, Walter, *The Aesthetic Movement in England*. London, 1882.

Haweis, Mrs H. R., *The Art of Beauty*. London, 1878.

Haweis, Mrs H. R., *Beautiful Houses*. London, 1882.

Lockwood and Glaister, *Art Embroidery*. London, 1878.

Loftie, Mrs, *The Dining Room*. London, 1878.

Orrinsmith, Mrs, *The Drawing Room*. London, 1878.

Robson, E. R., *School Architecture*. London, 1874.

Sedding, J. D., *Art and Handicraft*. London, 1893.

Smith, J. Moyr, *Ornamental Interiors*. London, 1887.

Spofford, Harriett Prescott, *Art Decoration Applied to Furniture*. New York, 1878.

Stevenson, J. J., *House Architecture*. London, 1880.

Wilde, Oscar, *Art and Decoration*. London, 1920.

Wilde, Oscar, *Decorative Art in America*. New York, 1906.

PERIODICALS

Architect. London, 1849–   .

Artist and Journal of Home Culture. London, 1880–'94.

Builder. London, 1842–   .

British Architect. Manchester, 1874–   .

Decoration. London, 1880–8.

Furniture Gazette. London, 1873–93.

Journal of Decorative Art. Manchester, 1881–   .

Magazine of Art. London, 1878–   .

Pottery Gazette and Glass Trades Review. London, 1879–   .

Punch. London, 1841–   .

Sylvia's Home Journal. London, 1878–91.

Index

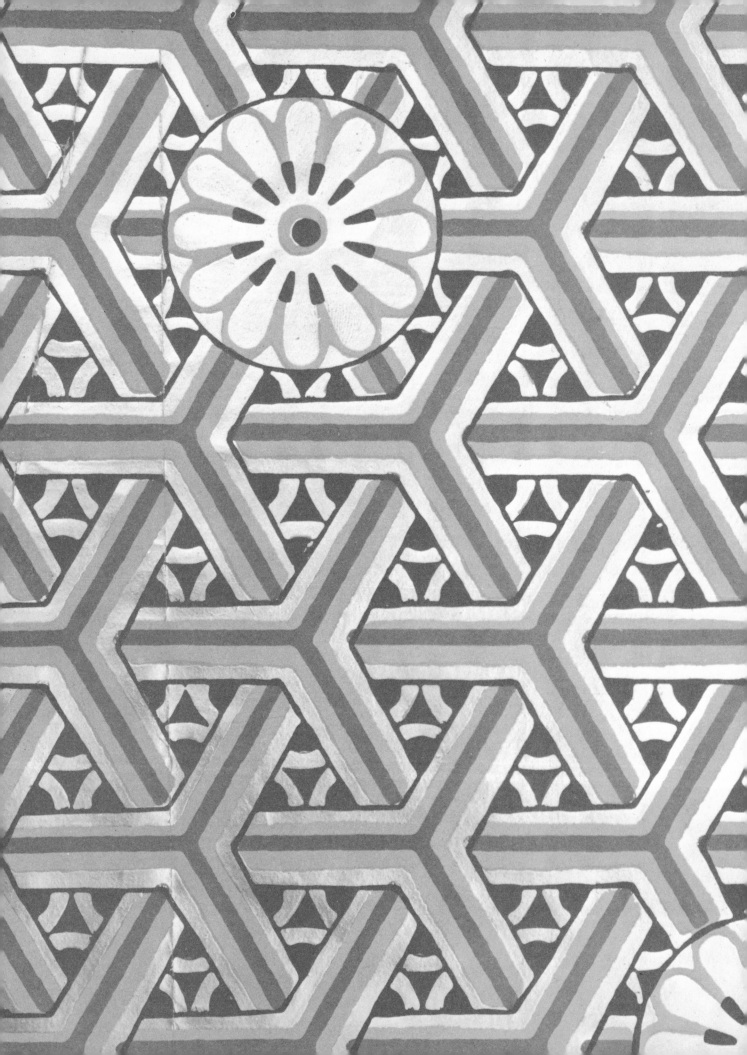